Fertility, Education and Macroeconomics: The Case of Japan

Masatoshi Jinno · Masaya Yasuoka
Editors

Fertility, Education and Macroeconomics: The Case of Japan

Springer

Editors
Masatoshi Jinno
Department of Economics
Nanzan University
Nagoya, Japan

Masaya Yasuoka
School of Economics
Kwansei Gakuin University
Nishinomiya, Hyogo, Japan

ISBN 978-981-95-1023-8 ISBN 978-981-95-1024-5 (eBook)
https://doi.org/10.1007/978-981-95-1024-5

This Springer imprint is published by the registered company Springer Nature Singapore Pte Ltd.
The registered company address is: 152 Beach Road, #21-01/04 Gateway East, Singapore 189721, Singapore

Preface

This book addresses the issue of declining birthrates and aging populations, which has become a significant problem in advanced countries, by utilizing an endogenous fertility model for its analysis. There are various problems associated with the issue of declining birthrates and aging populations, which include issues such as labor shortages and the sustainability of social security systems. While this book does cover themes related to the sustainability of social security systems, its primary purpose is to demonstrate how economic models can be formulated and analyzed to address the issue of declining birthrates and aging populations. There are numerous prior studies on this issue, including both theoretical and empirical research. However, this book primarily focuses on theoretical analysis and aims to serve as a handbook for those considering how to set up economic models to address the issue of declining birthrates and aging populations. For researchers engaged in theoretical analysis, it will provide guidance on how to set up their models. Similarly, for researchers conducting empirical studies, it will offer directions on model setup. Proper model setup is crucial for empirical research to avoid criticism of being "empirical without theory." By setting up models, the relationships between variables become clear, providing guidance for empirical analysis. Therefore, this book is also recommended for researchers conducting empirical studies who want to understand model setup.

The book is composed of a total of seven chapters, divided into a basic part and an applied part. The basic section consists of the following three chapters:

Chapter 1 Childcare Policies and Fertility
Chapter 2 Childcare Service and Fertility
Chapter 3 Pay-As-You-Go Pension, Fertility, and Educational Investment

These chapters deal with fundamental endogenous fertility models, focusing on analysis with simple model setups. They are intended to provide hints on how to set up models in practice. Chapter 1 not only covers the setup of endogenous fertility models and the effects of childcare support but also provides detailed guidance on solving economic models. Chapter 2 clarifies the differences between childcare services and childcare time, while Chap. 3 includes an analysis of very realistic models, considering educational investments in children and the pay-as-you-go pension system.

The applied part consists of the following four chapters:

Chapter 4 Fertility, Income Growth, and Inflation
Chapter 5 Fertility and Labor Share of Child Care Service
Chapter 6 Intergenerational Conflict in a Model of Endogenous Fertility
Chapter 7 The Effects of Admitting Immigrants on the Welfare of Each Generation of Natives

These chapters provide applied considerations based on fundamental models. Therefore, if you are interested in learning how to set up endogenous fertility models, the basic section should be sufficient. However, the applied section explores many intriguing themes. For instance, Chap. 4 examines the impact of monetary policy on fertility rates. Chapter 5 offers a more detailed model analysis of childcare services, building on the analysis in Chap. 2. Educational investment is a crucial aspect when considering endogenous fertility and is discussed in Chaps. 3, 4, and 7. Chapter 6 addresses the implementation of policies using political-economic equilibrium. While other chapters treat policy parameters as exogenous, Chap. 6 attempts to endogenize policy variables. Finally, Chap. 7 discusses the acceptance of immigrants. The applied section provides valuable themes for considering what policies are desirable in a society with declining birthrates and an aging population, such as Japan.

Furthermore, I had the opportunity to obtain research funding while studying this theme. Chapters 1 through 3 of this book are translations of the content from my previous work (in Japanese), *Economic Analysis of a Low Birthrate and Aging Society (Shoushikoureishakai no Keizaibunseki)* (K. G. University Press, 2021), published with the support of the Japan Society for the Promotion of Science's Grant-in-Aid for Publication of Scientific Research Results. I would also like to express my gratitude for the research conducted not only with the research funds from Kwansei Gakuin University but also with Grant-in-Aid for Scientific Research (C) (No. 22K01530 and 22K01547). Additionally, acknowledgments for research funding received in the past are included in the acknowledgments section of each chapter.

All the models presented in this book are unified under the framework of endogenous fertility models. One of the distinctive features of this book is that it illustrates the various analytical possibilities that can be explored within the context of endogenous fertility modeling.

Now, I would like to express my acknowledgments. During my graduate school years, I received significant support from Hideyuki Adachi, Takeshi Nakatani, Tamotsu Nakamura, and Takashi Oshio. I learned much under their guidance in graduate school, not only in preparing my doctoral dissertation but also in acquiring many essential skills for living in society. While there are many people to whom I am indebted, and listing them all would be extensive, I would especially like to mention those who supported me at the beginning of my research career: Nobuo Akai,

Kimiyoshi Kamada, Hisakazu Kato, Koji Kitaura, Makoto Hirazawa, Kazumasa Oguro, Toshiyuki Uemura, Mitoshi Yamaguchi, Akira Yakita, and Shinji Yamashige. Despite my insufficient analytical skills as a researcher at the time, they provided valuable comments and taught me the attitude necessary for being a researcher. I would also like to express my gratitude to Hideki Toya, who supported me during my undergraduate years. If I had not studied under him, I might not have become a researcher. Although he has since passed away, I regularly met with him during his lifetime, and discussing research life with him was both nerve-wracking and enjoyable. Tamotsu Nakamura was my seminar advisor during my graduate school years, but he passed away in 2024. Thanks to his guidance, I was able to write and present research papers. I had a dream of inviting him to a conference I would host someday and having him listen to my research papers but that dream will never come true.

Of course, I have also been supported by many others, and it has been my greatest joy to engage in joint research with numerous friends and junior colleagues. I believe that my ability to continue this research is due to the immense support from Kwansei Gakuin University, where I currently work, and from my colleagues there. My co-editor Masatoshi Jinno and co-author Masaya Shintani are also collaborators in this research. Lastly, I would like to express my gratitude to Juno Kawakami for considering this publication project, the anonymous referees for their feedback, and my family—Marina Yasuoka, Eishu Yasuoka, and Chio Yasuoka—for their support.

Nishinomiya, Japan
June 2025

On behalf of the editor and co-authors
Masaya Yasuoka

Contents

About the Editors

Masatoshi Jinno is a professor in the Faculty of Economics at Nanzan University. His research centers on immigration economics, public pension and social-security finance, and education economics. He has published articles in journals such as *FinanzArchiv: Public Finance Analysis*, *Demographic Research*, *The Singapore Economic Review*, and *The International Review of Economics*. He earned a Ph.D. in Economics from Nagoya University and holds a B.A. in Foreign Studies from Osaka University of Foreign Studies.

Masaya Yasuoka is a professor at the School of Economics, Kwansei Gakuin University. His main areas of research interest are public finance, social security and macroeconomics. He has published papers in scholarly journals including *Economics Letters Economic Modelling*, *International Review of Economics* and *Journal of the Economics of Ageing*. Professor Yasuoka received a B.A. in Economics from Nagoya City University and a Ph.D. in Economics from Kobe University.

About the Editors

Chapter 1
Childcare Policies and Fertility

Masaya Yasuoka

1 Introduction

In advanced countries, the trend of declining birthrates and aging populations is progressing, with Japan particularly advanced in this regard. The elderly population, defined as those aged 65 and older, constitutes the aging rate, which represents the proportion of elderly people relative to the total population. In Japan, this rate exceeds one in four people, the highest in the world. On the other hand, the total fertility rate, which is the average number of children a woman will have in her lifetime, remains around 1.3. As a nation, the Japanese government aims to implement proactive childcare support policies to increase the total fertility rate (see Fig. 1).

The reason why declining birthrates and aging populations are problematic is that social security systems, including pension schemes, are primarily funded by contributions from the working-age population. As the size of the working-age population decreases, overall tax revenue and social insurance premium income will stagnate. Consequently, it will become difficult to provide sufficient social security benefits to the elderly, necessitating either benefit cuts or increased burdens on both the working-age and elderly populations.

Childcare support policies exist in various forms. Cash benefits include child allowances and single-parent allowances. Child allowances are provided as a monthly payment per child. Single-parent allowances are given to households below a certain income level. There are also in-kind benefits. For example, subsidies are provided to daycare centers and kindergartens where parents send their children. Additionally, depending on the municipality, there are subsidies for children's medical expenses, where parents only need to pay the portion not covered by the subsidy when their children receive medical care. In-kind benefits are provided by offering services at

M. Yasuoka (✉)
School of Economics, Kwansei Gakuin University, Nishinomiya, Japan
e-mail: yasuoka@kwansei.ac.jp

M. Jinno and M. Yasuoka (eds.), *Fertility, Education and Macroeconomics: The Case of Japan*, https://doi.org/10.1007/978-981-95-1024-5_1

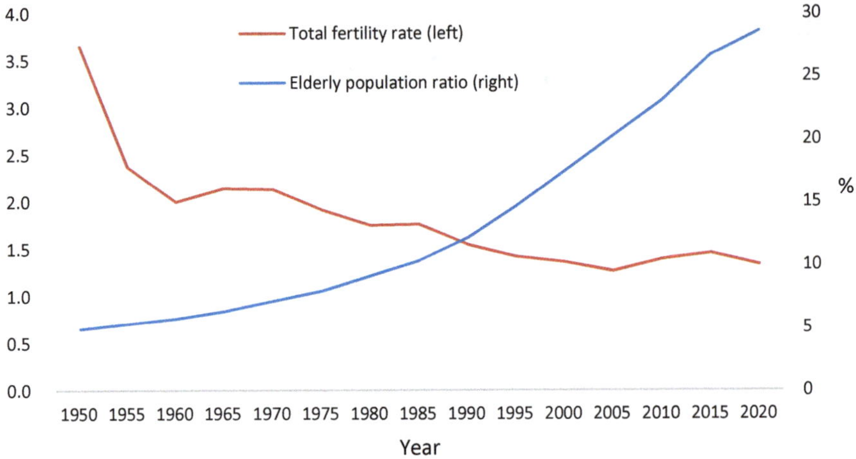

Fig. 1 Trend of total fertility rate and elderly population ratio in Japan. *Source* Ministry of Health, Labour and Welfare of Japan (2023)

a low cost rather than giving money directly to individuals. Subsidies for education can be considered one form of in-kind benefits.

Despite the existence of various benefits, this chapter aims to explain how a certain type of cash benefit provided to households with children affects the birthrate. Specifically, it examines the effect of child allowances. Figure 2 shows the ratio of social expenditure on family-related benefits to GDP in some countries.

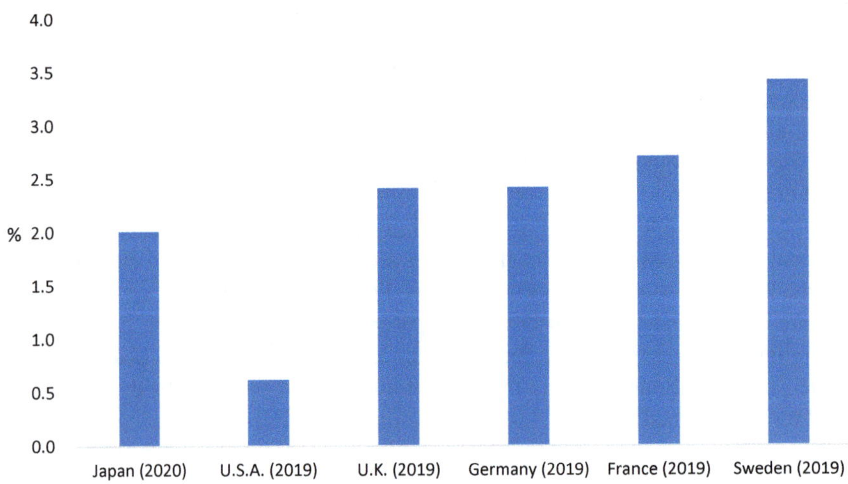

Fig. 2 The ratio of social expenditure on family-related benefits to GDP. *Source* Children and Families Agency, Government of Japan (2024)

For the model setting, we use an endogenous fertility model where households choose the number of children to maximize their utility. There are many studies that consider childcare support policies using an endogenous fertility model. For example, an analysis in a small open economy (where interest rates and wage rates are held constant) was conducted by van Groezen, Leers, and Meijdam (2003). In contrast, studies by Oshio (2001) and van Groezen and Meijdam (2008) considered closed economy models where interest rates and wage rates change due to capital accumulation. Elsewhere, Yasuoka (2006) analyzed the impact of childcare support policies on the birthrate in a closed economy mainly through numerical simulations. Yasuoka's model differs from the others as it considers the choice of tax sources, taking into account not only income tax but also consumption tax.

Comparing the effects of policies in closed and open economies is important. In a closed economy, the increased tax burden for the policy not only directly reduces households' disposable income, negatively affecting the number of children, but also leads to reduced savings due to the decrease in disposable income. As a result, corporate investment decreases, leading to a drop in productivity. This, in turn, reduces households' labor income, which further negatively impacts the number of children.

To thoroughly understand these dynamics, in the following sections, I will first establish a simplified model based on existing literature, such as the works of van Groezen, Leers, and Meijdam (2003) and Yasuoka and Goto (2011), to analyze childcare support policies in a small open economy. Subsequently, a closed economy model will be developed to highlight the differing impacts of such policies when international financial flows are restricted, following models based on the work of Oshio (2001), van Groezen and Meijdam (2008) and Yasuoka and Goto (2015).

Through these models, I aim to provide a comprehensive analysis of how childcare support policies can influence birthrates in different economic contexts, offering insights into the most effective strategies for addressing declining birthrates and aging populations.

2 Model

First, let's set up the simplest model for analyzing childcare support policies. In this model, there are households and the government. Individuals in households live through two periods: youth and old age. Life is roughly divided into these two periods. In youth, individuals perform one unit of inelastic labor and earn a wage w. This wage income is allocated to youth consumption $c_{y,t}$, childcare expenses, and savings s_t for old age consumption $c_{o,t+1}$.

The cost of raising one child is denoted as z, and the benefit received per child from childcare support policies is denoted as q. Specifically, this can be thought of as a child allowance, but it could also be considered an in-kind benefit. If the number of children is n_t, the expenditure for childcare is $(z - q)n_t$. The funding for the childcare support policy is collected from labor income, with a tax rate denoted as τ. Note that t indicates the period, and individuals in their youth in period t become elderly in period $t+1$. The budget constraint in youth is expressed as follows:

$$c_{y,t} + (z - q)n_t + s_t = (1 - \tau)w. \tag{1}$$

Next, regarding behavior in old age, individuals do not work, and their consumption is financed by the principal and interest of their savings. The budget constraint in old age is expressed as follows:

$$c_{o,t+1} = (1 + r)s_t. \tag{2}$$

Here, r is the interest rate. By expressing s_t as $s_t = \frac{c_{o,t+1}}{1+r}$ from (2) and substituting it into (1), the lifetime budget constraint can be expressed as follows:

$$c_{y,t} + (z - q)n_t + \frac{c_{o,t+1}}{1 + r} = (1 - \tau)w. \tag{3}$$

If, unlike in this model, individuals can choose their working hours and leisure time, rather than spending a fixed amount of time on inelastic labor, an increase in the income tax rate would additionally affect income by reducing the time spent working.[1] How taxes are levied can greatly influence the results obtained, so caution is necessary.

Now, let's move on to the utility function u_t, which we assume as follows[2]:

$$u_t = \alpha \ln n_t + \beta \ln c_{y,t} + (1 - \alpha - \beta)\ln c_{o,t+1}, \quad 0 < \alpha < 1, \quad 0 < \beta < 1, \quad \alpha + \beta < 1. \tag{4}$$

The utility function is set to endogenously determine consumption and the number of children. Individuals in households choose each allocation, such as consumption and the number of children, to maximize the utility function (4) while satisfying the budget constraint (3).

The law of diminishing marginal utility applies to this utility function. To examine this in more detail, let's extract $\ln n_t$ and illustrate it graphically.

Figure 3 illustrates the law of diminishing marginal utility for the number of children. When the number of children is low, increasing the number of children can significantly increase utility. However, when there is already a considerable number of children, further increasing the number of children results in only a small additional increase in utility. This additional increase in utility is called marginal utility, and the phenomenon where this additional increase in utility becomes smaller is known as the law of diminishing marginal utility. The same law applies to consumption in both

[1] The decrease in the after-tax wage rate due to income tax reduces the opportunity cost of leisure, which in turn affects the amount of time supplied for labor. In this model, however, the labor supply time is considered fixed.

[2] This is known as a logarithmic utility function, which is commonly used in economic model settings. It should be noted that even if the utility function is set as a Cobb–Douglas type, $u_t = n_t^{\alpha} c_{y,t}^{\beta} c_{o,t+1}^{1-\alpha-\beta}$, the results obtained would be the same.

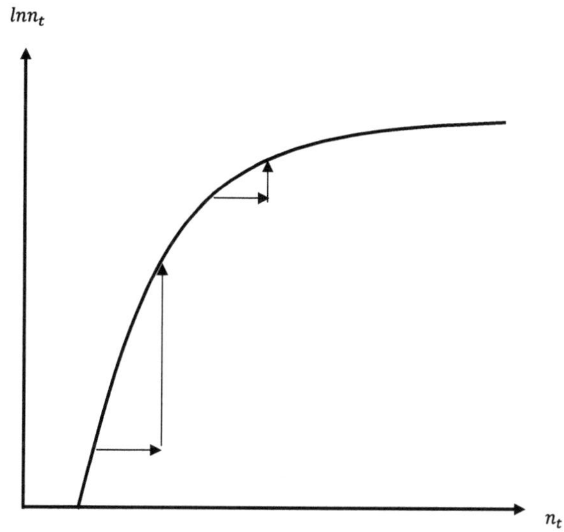

Fig. 3 Rule of decrease in marginal utility

youth and old age. Considering the additional increase in utility, individuals within a household decide on the number of children and the allocation of consumption.[3]

Now, let's find the allocation that maximizes the utility function (4) under the budget constraint Eq. (3). For this purpose, we can use a method called the Lagrange multiplier method. The Lagrangian function L is set as follows:

$$L = \alpha \ln n_t + \beta \ln c_{y,t} + (1-\alpha-\beta)\ln c_{o,t+1} + \lambda\left((1-\tau)w - c_{y,t} - (z-q)n_t - \frac{c_{o,t+1}}{1+r}\right). \tag{5}$$

Here, let's consider the constraint condition as $(1-\tau)w - c_{y,t} - (z-q)n_t - \frac{c_{o,t+1}}{1+r} = 0$. We add the Lagrange multiplier λ to the utility function, resulting in the Lagrangian function. This function is differentiated with respect to n_t, $c_{y,t}$, $c_{o,t+1}$, λ, and each partial derivative is set to zero.

$$\frac{\partial L}{\partial n_t} = \frac{\alpha}{n_t} - \lambda(z-q) = 0 \rightarrow \frac{\alpha}{\lambda} = (z-q)n_t \tag{6}$$

$$\frac{\partial L}{\partial c_{y,t}} = \frac{\beta}{c_{y,t}} - \lambda = 0 \rightarrow \frac{\beta}{\lambda} = c_{y,t} \tag{7}$$

[3] In economic analysis, logarithmic utility functions are often used. The reasons they are often used are that, as shown in Fig. 3, the law of diminishing marginal utility holds true, and an interior solution (where no allocation is zero and all allocations are positive) can be obtained. Additionally, as will be seen in subsequent calculations, the number of children and consumption can each be derived as a formula representing a certain proportion of income, making the results easy to express explicitly. Furthermore, as will be discussed later, there is the advantage of these functions being easier to handle when endogenizing capital accumulation and conducting long-term analysis.

$$\frac{\partial L}{\partial c_{o,t+1}} = \frac{1-\alpha-\beta}{c_{o,t+1}} - \frac{\lambda}{1+r} = 0 \rightarrow \frac{1-\alpha-\beta}{\lambda} = \frac{c_{o,t+1}}{1+r} \tag{8}$$

$$\frac{\partial L}{\partial \lambda} = (1-\tau)w - c_{y,t} - (z-q)n_t - \frac{c_{o,t+1}}{1+r} = 0 \tag{9}$$

These are called the first-order conditions, which are the necessary conditions for the optimal solution. By substituting (6) through (8) into (3), we obtain the following equation:

$$\frac{1}{\lambda} = (1-\tau)w. \tag{10}$$

Therefore, by substituting (10) into (6)–(8), the number of children and consumption are determined as follows:

$$n_t = \frac{\alpha(1-\tau)w}{z-q}, \tag{11}$$

$$c_{y,t} = \beta(1-\tau)w, \tag{12}$$

$$c_{o,t+1} = (1+r)(1-\alpha-\beta)(1-\tau)w. \tag{13}$$

The number of children and consumption are determined proportionally based on income $(1-\tau)w$ and the parameters of the utility function (known as preference parameters). For example, α is the preference parameter for the utility derived from the number of children; as this parameter increases, the number of children also increases.

Next, let's consider the government's budget constraint. The government collects income tax from the young generation and provides benefits to them. The number of young people is N_t, and if each young individual has n_t children, the necessary cost for the government's childcare support policy is qN_tn_t. On the other hand, the amount of labor income tax collected from the young generation is $\tau N_t w$. If the government implements a balanced budget policy, the following equation holds:

$$\tau N_t w = qN_t n_t \rightarrow \tau w = qn_t. \tag{14}$$

By substituting this equation into (11), we can obtain the following equation:

$$n_t = \frac{\alpha w}{z-(1-\alpha)q}. \tag{15}$$

Therefore, it is evident that increasing the childcare support benefit q will lead to an increase in the number of children n_t. In this intuitive manner, we have derived the effects of childcare support policies by constructing and analyzing an economic model.

This model is quite simplified. Next, we will take a step further and consider childcare support policies within a model that endogenizes capital accumulation.

3 Capital Accumulation Model

The previous model was a small open economy model where the interest rate and wage rate were treated as constant and exogenous. In reality, household savings determine investments, which in turn influence the level of capital stock as a factor of production. Therefore, we should consider this effect. Here, individuals within households still live through two periods, young and old age, as before. Although not explicitly explained previously, such a model is known as an overlapping generations model, in which each period features the coexistence of both young and old generations (Fig. 4).

Let the wage rate in period t be w_t and the interest rate be r_t. In this case, the individual's lifetime budget constraint Eq. (3) is modified as follows:

$$c_{y,t} + (z - q)n_t + \frac{c_{o,t+1}}{1 + r_t} = (1 - \tau)w_t. \tag{16}$$

Then, the optimal allocations (11)–(13) are adjusted to include w_t and r_t for the wage rate and interest rate, respectively.

Next, when considering the wage rate and interest rate in a closed economy, it is necessary to take into account the behavior of firms. So far, the economic model included two agents: households and the government. Now, we add firms as another agent. First, firms produce goods and services by using capital stock K_t and labor L_t as input factors. The output level is Y_t. The relationship between these input factors and the output level is described by the production function. Here, we assume the following Cobb–Douglas production function:

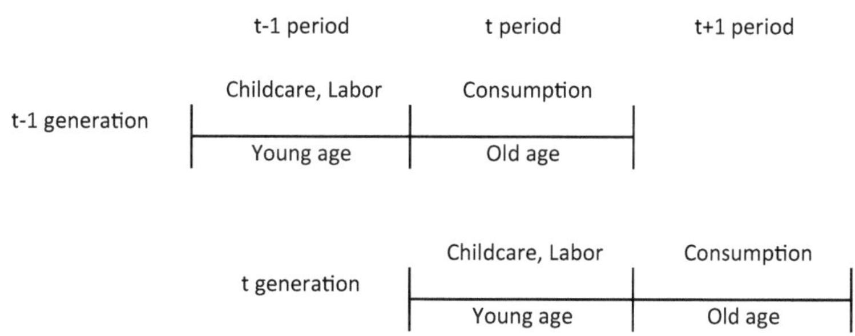

Fig. 4 Overlapping generations model

$$Y_t = K_t^{\theta} L_t^{1-\theta}, \quad 0 < \theta < 1. \tag{17}$$

Next, let's consider the profit-maximizing behavior of firms. Assuming the price of goods and services is 1, the revenue from production is Y_t, and the costs of production include payments to workers, $w_t L_t$, and the cost of borrowing capital stock, $(1 + r_t)K_t$. Here, it is assumed that capital is completely depreciated after one period. In other words, if capital is rented and used for production for one period, it is fully depreciated. Therefore, the repayment for borrowed capital includes the capital itself, making the cost $(1 + r_t)K_t$ rather than just $r_t K_t$. This type of production function is known as a Cobb–Douglas production function, which is frequently used in economic analysis.

Firms maximize their profit π_t. Profit can be formulated as follows:

$$\pi_t = K_t^{\theta} L_t^{1-\theta} - (1 + r_t)K_t - w_t L_t. \tag{18}$$

Firms determine the levels of capital stock K_t and labor L_t to maximize their profit. Given the shape of the firm's production function, we can illustrate the following diagram.

Figure 5 illustrates the labor input that maximizes profit when the capital stock is fixed. As labor input increases, the firm's output also increases, but the rate of increase slows down progressively, which is known as the diminishing marginal productivity. On the other hand, costs increase by w_t for each additional unit of labor input. Therefore, the optimal level of labor input is determined where the additional cost of w_t for one unit of labor input equals the marginal productivity of labor (the slope of the tangent line indicated by the dashed line on the production function curve). A similar approach can be applied to determine the optimal level of capital stock.

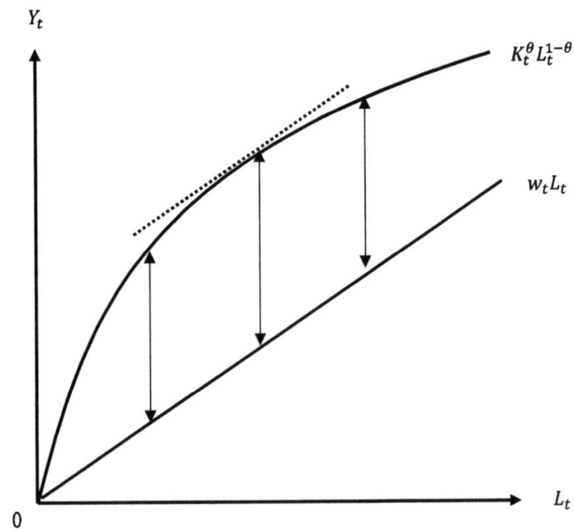

Fig. 5 Profit maximization. *Note* The slope of the tangent line represents the marginal productivity of labor, that is, it indicates how many units of output will increase with a one-unit increase in labor input

Based on the above, by differentiating π_t with respect to K_t and L_t and setting these derivatives to zero, the wage rate w_t and the interest rate r_t can be determined as follows:

$$\frac{\partial \pi_t}{\partial L_t} = (1-\theta)\frac{K_t^{\theta}}{L_t^{\theta}} - w_t = 0 \rightarrow w_t = (1-\theta)k_t^{\theta}, \tag{19}$$

$$\frac{\partial \pi_t}{\partial K_t} = \theta\frac{L_t^{1-\theta}}{K_t^{1-\theta}} - 1 + r_t = 0 \rightarrow 1 + r_t = \theta k_t^{\theta-1}. \tag{20}$$

$k_t = \frac{K_t}{L_t}$ is defined. This is a capital labor ratio or capital stock per capita.

In a small open economy, the interest rate and wage rate are considered constant, based on the assumption that the domestic interest rate (20) is equal to the world interest rate. In this scenario, the interest rate is fixed by the world interest rate, thereby fixing the capital stock as well. Consequently, the wage rate is also fixed, as determined by (19). Therefore, in a small open economy, the fixed interest rate and wage rate are given by the world interest rate and Eqs. (19) and (20). Based on the above, the number of children, as indicated in (15), is shown as:

$$n_t = \frac{\alpha w_t}{z - (1-\alpha)q}. \tag{21}$$

Next, in a closed economy model, we must consider the dynamic equation of capital stock k_t. In the capital market of period t, savings equal investments. Consequently, investments determine the capital stock for the next period,$t+1$. Once the level of capital stock is determined, the interest rate is also determined. The equilibrium equation of the capital market can be expressed as follows:

$$K_{t+1} = N_t s_t \rightarrow n_t k_{t+1} = s_t \rightarrow n_t k_{t+1} = (1-\tau)w_t - (z-q)n_t - c_{y,t} \tag{22}$$

$n_t = \frac{N_{t+1}}{N_t}$ is given.[4] By substituting (11) and (12) into (22), the dynamic equation of capital stock is derived as follows:

$$k_{t+1} = \frac{(1-\alpha-\beta)(z-q)}{\alpha}. \tag{23}$$

As this equation shows, the level of capital stock remains constant over time. Since it is not dependent on time, we will denote it as k. Furthermore, it can be observed that an increase in the childcare support benefit q leads to a decrease in the capital stock k. By differentiating k with respect to q, this can be demonstrated as follows:

[4] Here, since the capital stock is fully depreciated within one period, savings and investment in period t are equal, and investment in period t is equal to the capital stock in period $t+1$. Therefore, we have $K_{t+1} = N_t s_t$. Here, N_t is the population size of the young generation in period t, and N_{t+1} is the population size of the young generation in period $t+1$, with their ratio representing the birth rate.

$$\frac{dk}{dq} = -\frac{1-\alpha-\beta}{\alpha} < 0. \tag{24}$$

It can be observed here that the capital stock decreases. This is an intuitive result because the effect of increased childcare support benefits leads to an increase in the number of children, which, when viewed as the capital stock per capita (capital stock divided by population size), results in a decrease.

Next, let's examine the change in the number of children. Considering (19), Eq. (21) can be expressed as follows[5]:

$$(z-(1-\alpha)q)n = \alpha(1-\theta)k^{\theta}. \tag{25}$$

Here, we perform the total differentiation as follows:

$$zdn = (1-\alpha)ndq + \alpha\theta(1-\theta)k^{\theta-1}dk. \tag{26}$$

By substituting $dk = -\frac{1-\alpha-\beta}{\alpha}dq$ from (24), the change in the number of children can be expressed as follows:

$$\frac{dn}{dq} = \frac{(1-\alpha-\theta)n}{z}. \tag{27}$$

The number of children does not necessarily increase with childcare support benefits. If $1-\alpha-\theta > 0$, the number of children increases, but if $1-\alpha-\theta < 0$, the number of children decreases. This indicates whether the effect of the reduction in capital stock due to policy is large or small. When the capital stock decreases, the wage rate also decreases, which leads to a reduction in the number of children. This is shown by the term $\alpha\theta(1-\theta)k^{\theta-1}dk$ in (26). On the other hand, childcare support benefits directly increase the number of children, as indicated by the term $(1-\alpha)ndq$ in (26). The effect of childcare support benefits is determined by which of these effects is larger, demonstrating that in a closed economy, childcare support policies are not necessarily effective as a countermeasure against declining birth rates.

[5] The capital stock remains constant over time, and since the number of children does not affect the capital stock, it also remains constant and does not depend on time. Here, when performing the total differentiation, we consider $q = \tau = 0$, meaning that we evaluate and differentiate under the condition $q = \tau = 0$.

4 Financing Through Consumption Tax

Let's consider the case where childcare support benefits are funded through a consumption tax instead of an income tax. In recent years, in Japan, an increase in the consumption tax has been advocated to fund social security benefits. Therefore, in the future, the consumption tax could be considered a potential source of funding for such policies.

Let the consumption tax rate be τ_c, and assume it is levied on both consumption in the young period and consumption in the old period. However, let's assume that the consumption tax is not levied on childcare expenditures. This is because imposing a consumption tax on childcare expenditures would weaken the effect of childcare support benefits, and this assumption eliminates that impact. Moreover, considering that childcare expenditures include costs for childcare and education, which are often exempt from taxation in Japan, it is reasonable to assume that consumption tax is not levied on childcare expenditures.

The lifetime budget constraint under the consumption tax can be expressed as follows:

$$(1+\tau_c)c_{y,t} + (z-q)n_t + \frac{(1+\tau_c)c_{o,t+1}}{1+r_{t+1}} = w_t. \tag{28}$$

The allocation that maximizes the utility function (4) under the budget constraint (28) is given as follows:

$$n_t = \frac{\alpha w_t}{z-q}, \tag{29}$$

$$c_{y,t} = \frac{\beta w_t}{1+\tau_c}, \tag{30}$$

$$c_{o,t+1} = \frac{(1+r_{t+1})(1-\alpha-\beta)w_t}{1+\tau_c}. \tag{31}$$

The government's budget constraint is shown as follows. Note that the first term on the left side represents the consumption tax revenue from the young generation's consumption, the second term on the left side represents the consumption tax revenue from the old generation's consumption, and the right side represents the childcare support benefits:

$$N_t\tau_c c_{y,t} + N_{t-1}\tau_c c_{o,t} = N_t q n_t \rightarrow \tau_c c_{y,t} + \tau_c\frac{c_{o,t}}{n_{t-1}} = qn_t. \tag{32}$$

N_t represents the population size of the young generation in period t, and N_{t-1} represents the population size of the old generation in period t (the young generation in period $t-1$), with $\frac{N_t}{N_{t-1}} = n_{t-1}$.

The dynamic equation of capital is given as follows:

$$K_{t+1} = N_t s_t \rightarrow n_t k_{t+1} = s_t \rightarrow n_t k_{t+1} = w_t - (z - q)n_t - (1 + \tau_c)c_{y,t}. \tag{33}$$

$n_t = \frac{N_{t+1}}{N_t}$ is given. By substituting (29) and (30) into (33), the dynamic equation for capital stock is derived as follows,

$$k_{t+1} = \frac{(1 - \alpha - \beta)(z - q)}{\alpha}. \tag{34}$$

Even in the case of a consumption tax, the level of capital stock remains constant over time. Similarly, as in the case of an income tax, it can be observed that an increase in childcare support benefits q leads to a decrease in capital stock k. Differentiating k with respect to q yields the same result as in (24). This is also due to the direct increase in the number of children from childcare support benefits, which increases the population size and consequently reduces the capital stock allocated per capita.

Next, let's examine the changes in the number of children. Equation (29) can be expressed as follows[6]:

$$(z - q)n = \alpha(1 - \theta)k^{\theta}. \tag{35}$$

By total differentiation, the following equation is derived,[7]

$$zdn - ndq = \alpha\theta(1 - \theta)k^{\theta - 1}dk. \tag{36}$$

Substituting (24) into (36), we can obtain $\frac{dn}{dq}$ as follows[8]:

$$\frac{dn}{dq} = \frac{(1 - \theta)n}{z} > 0. \tag{37}$$

Since $0 < \theta < 1$, the childcare support benefits funded by a consumption tax will inevitably increase the number of children. This contrasts with the case of an income tax, which reduces the number of children by directly decreasing household disposable income. As the ratio of each consumption allocation is determined by the preference parameters of the utility function, considering a logarithmic utility function, the following ratio remains unchanged even with the consideration of a consumption tax:

$(z - q)n_t : (1 + \tau_c)c_{y,t} : \frac{(1+\tau_c)c_{o,t+1}}{1+r_{t+1}} = \alpha : \beta : 1 - \alpha - \beta$. Therefore, if the proportion of $(1 + \tau_c)c_{y,t}$ to income is fixed, an increase in τ_c will directly lead to a decrease in $c_{y,t}$. Additionally, even in the case of a child allowance financed by a consumption tax, the capital stock decreases, which in turn lowers the wage levels

[6] The capital stock remains constant over time, and since the number of children does not affect the capital stock, it also remains constant over time.

[7] Please notify the total differentiation at $q = 0$.

[8] We obtain (37) by considering the wage rate $w = (1 - \theta)k^{\theta}$ and the capital accumulation $n = \frac{(1-\alpha-\beta)w}{k}$.

individuals receive. This has the effect of reducing the number of children, but it was found that this effect is smaller than the effect of the childcare support benefits.

5 Income Proportional Childcare Cost

In the previous model, the childcare cost per child,z, was considered constant. Therefore, even if household wage rates change due to the level of capital accumulation, the constant childcare cost z can result in cases where the childcare cost becomes relatively higher or lower.

However, if we consider childcare costs z to include expenses for childcare services or educational investments, and take into account the wage levels of those providing these services, it is natural to consider childcare costs z as proportional to wages. In this section, we will consider cases where such childcare costs are wage-proportional.

$$z_t = \overline{z}w_t, 0 < \overline{z} \tag{38}$$

Furthermore, to ensure that the level of childcare support benefits does not become relatively lower due to changes in wage rates, we will set the benefit formula as follows:

$$q_t = \overline{q}w_t, 0 < \overline{q}. \tag{39}$$

If the wage level w_t increases, the childcare cost z_t will also rise, but the childcare support benefit q_t will increase as well. In this situation, among the allocations (11)–(13) that maximize the utility function (4), only (11) changes and is shown as follows:

$$n_t = \frac{\alpha(1-\tau)w_t}{z_t - q_t} = \frac{\alpha(1-\tau)}{\overline{z} - \overline{q}}. \tag{40}$$

Then, using Eq. (14), the government's budget constraint can be expressed as follows (in the case of income tax):

$$\tau N_t w_t = q_t N_t n_t \rightarrow \tau w_t = q_t n_t \rightarrow \tau = \overline{q} n_t. \tag{41}$$

Therefore, based on (40) and (41), the number of children can be expressed as follows:

$$n = \frac{\alpha}{\overline{z} - (1-\alpha)\overline{q}}. \tag{42}$$

Since it remains constant over time, there is no subscript to represent time. From this equation, it can be seen that increasing the childcare support benefit level $\overline{q}$ will invariably increase the number of children. The reason is intuitive: there is no effect of a decrease in the capital stock leading to a reduction in the wage rate. To elaborate further, as the childcare cost in the denominator is also proportional to the wage, the effect of the capital stock reduction associated with the increase in $\overline{q}$ lowers the childcare cost per child, which in turn has the effect of increasing the number of children. The effect of the reduction in disposable household income due to the decrease in capital stock is exactly offset by the reduction in childcare costs, resulting in the number of children increasing due to the childcare support benefit.

Next, let's look at the impact on the capital stock. The dynamic equation of the capital stock, obtained by substituting (38) and (39) into (22), is expressed as follows:

$$n_t k_{t+1} = (1-\tau)w_t - (z_t - q_t)n_t - c_{y,t}. \tag{43}$$

By substituting (12) and (40) into (43), the dynamic equation of the capital stock is derived as follows:

$$k_{t+1} = \frac{(1-\alpha-\beta)(1-\tau)w_t}{n_t} = \frac{(1-\alpha-\beta)(\overline{z}-\overline{q})(1-\theta)k_t^{\theta}}{\alpha}. \tag{44}$$

This equation shows the dynamics of the capital stock. For example, in period t, the capital stock k_t is already given, and based on this, the capital stock for the next period k_{t+1} is determined. It can be illustrated as follows:

If the capital stock is given as k_0, it will increase to k_1 in the next period according to (44). Then, in the following period, it will again increase to k_2 according to (44). Ultimately, it will increase to k and then stop. The change in the capital stock will cease over time. This state is called the steady state. When conducting long-term policy analysis, this steady state is often analyzed. On the other hand, for short-term policy analysis, the analysis is often conducted either during the transition process until convergence to the steady state or by halting the movement of the capital stock.

Additionally, even if the capital stock is given at a level far from the steady-state capital stock, it will converge to the steady-state capital stock over time. This is referred to as stability. When analyzing in the steady state, the analysis is meaningless unless the system eventually reaches this state in the long term. Therefore, it is necessary to check for stability and demonstrate that the system is stable, confirming that it reaches the steady-state as a long-term equilibrium. As seen in Fig. 6, stability is apparent, but it can be shown to be stable by differentiating (44) as follows:

$$\frac{dk_{t+1}}{dk_t} = \frac{\theta(1-\alpha-\beta)(\overline{z}-\overline{q})(1-\theta)k_t^{\theta-1}}{\alpha}. \tag{45}$$

Considering (44) and $k_{t+1} = k_t = k$, the steady state capital stock k is derived as follows:

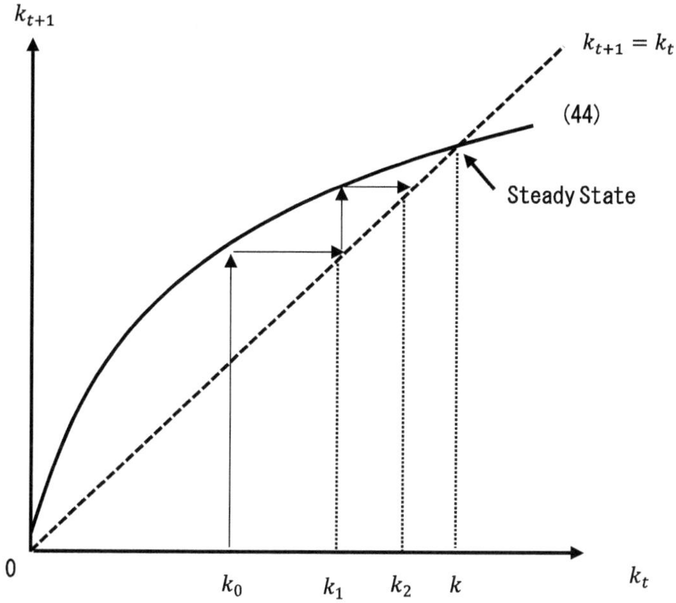

Fig. 6 Dynamics of capital stock

$$k = \frac{(1-\alpha-\beta)(\overline{z}-\overline{q})(1-\theta)k^{\theta}}{\alpha} \rightarrow k = \left(\frac{(1-\alpha-\beta)(\overline{z}-\overline{q})(1-\theta)}{\alpha}\right)^{\frac{1}{1-\theta}}. \tag{46}$$

Therefore, by substituting the steady-state capital stock (46) into (45), the stability of the steady state can be demonstrated as follows:

$$\frac{dk_{t+1}}{dk_t} = \theta. \tag{47}$$

If $-1 < \frac{dk_{t+1}}{dk_t} < 1$, the steady state is stable. Because of $0 < \theta < 1$, the steady state is stable.

Next, we want to examine how the steady-state capital stock changes due to childcare support benefits. As shown in (46), an increase in the level of childcare support benefits $\overline{q}$ decreases the steady-state capital stock k. This can also be demonstrated by differentiating with respect to $\overline{q} = 0$ as follows:

$$\begin{aligned}\frac{dk}{d\overline{q}} &= -\frac{1}{1-\theta}\frac{(1-\alpha-\beta)(1-\theta)}{\alpha}\left(\frac{(1-\alpha-\beta)(\overline{z}-\overline{q})(1-\theta)}{a}\right)^{\frac{1}{1-\theta}-1}\\ &= -\frac{k}{(1-\theta)\overline{z}} < 0.\end{aligned} \tag{48}$$

By adjusting the childcare cost per child in this way, the childcare support benefits funded by income tax will invariably result in an increase in the number of children.

Next, let's examine the case of a consumption tax. Similar to the previous scenario, if a consumption tax is not applied to childcare expenses but is levied on consumption during both the young and old age periods, and the revenue is allocated to childcare support benefits, the number of children indicated in (29) is modified as follows:

$$n_t = \frac{\alpha w_t}{z_t - q_t} = \frac{\alpha}{\overline{z} - \overline{q}}. \tag{49}$$

Therefore, the level of childcare support benefits $\overline{q}$ will invariably increase the number of children. Additionally, since the steady-state capital stock is given by (44), the level of capital stock will also decrease due to the policy.

6 In-Kind Childcare Support Model

So far, we have considered childcare support benefits provided to individuals. However, in reality, there are forms of childcare support other than individual benefits, such as the government's provision of childcare services, facilities, and hospitals. Yasuoka (2007) analyzed the impact of such support mechanisms on the number of children. Let's simplify that model into a small open economy model for explanation.

First, regarding the number of children, we assume the following birth rate function and determine the number of children using the following function:

$$n_t = g_t^{\delta} x_t^{1-\delta}, \quad 0 < \delta < 1. \tag{50}$$

g_t and x_t denote the amount of public services available per household and childcare goods and services invested per household, respectively.

Let the utility function u_t be (4). By substituting (50) into (4), we obtain the following equation:

$$\begin{aligned} u_t &= \alpha\delta \ln g_t + \alpha(1-\delta)\ln x_t \\ &\quad + \beta \ln c_{y,t} + (1-\alpha-\beta)\ln c_{o,t+1}, \quad 0 < \alpha < 1, \quad 0 < \beta < 1, \quad \alpha + \beta < 1. \end{aligned} \tag{51}$$

In their youth, individuals invest in childcare goods and services and consume $c_{y,t}$, while in old age, they consume $c_{o,t+1}$. The funding for public services is collected at a tax rate τ on wage income from the younger generation. At this time, the lifetime budget constraint for an individual household is as follows:

$$c_{y,t} + zx_t + \frac{c_{o,t+1}}{1+r} = (1-\tau)w. \tag{52}$$

Here, z is the price per unit of childcare goods and services. Based on the allocation that maximizes the utility function (51) under the budget constraint (52), the demand for childcare goods and services x_t is given as follows:

$$x = \frac{\alpha(1-\delta)(1-\tau)w}{z(1-\alpha\delta)}. \tag{53}$$

The government budget constraint is shown as follows:

$$N_t g_t = N_t \tau w \rightarrow g = \tau w. \tag{54}$$

Because of substituting (53) and (54) into (50), we can obtain the number of children.

$$n = \tau^{\delta}(1-\tau)^{1-\delta}\left(\frac{\alpha(1-\delta)}{z(1-\alpha\delta)}\right)^{1-\delta} w \tag{55}$$

The tax rate to maximize the number of children is given as follows:

$$\frac{dn}{d\tau} = \left(\delta\tau^{\delta-1}(1-\tau)^{1-\delta} - (1-\delta)\tau^{\delta}(1-\tau)^{-\delta}\right)\left(\frac{\alpha(1-\delta)}{z(1-\alpha\delta)}\right)^{1-\delta} w = 0 \rightarrow \tau = \delta. \tag{56}$$

Therefore, the number of children is maximized when the tax rate $\tau = \delta$. If the tax rate is set too high, although the supply of public services increases, the investment in childcare goods and services decreases. Hence, there is an optimal tax rate that maximizes the number of children.

However, the optimal policy might not be to maximize the number of children. Of course, in addressing the declining birthrate, policies that can increase the number of children as much as possible would be welcome. However, if such policies result in a substantial tax burden, they cannot be considered desirable. This is because a significant tax burden would greatly reduce consumption and substantially lower the level of utility. Therefore, the optimal policy should aim to maximize the level of utility. In the next section, I will present the socially desirable number of children as a policy goal.

7 Optimal Number of Children

In the work of van Groezen and Meijdam (2008) and Yasuoka and Goto (2015), we seek to determine the number of children and the level of consumption that maximize the social welfare function, which is the sum of the utilities of each generation, and to demonstrate that policies can achieve the number of children that maximize the social welfare function. Following the methods used in these research papers, I aim to derive the socially desirable number of children.

First, the social welfare function W is defined as follows[9]:

$$\begin{aligned} W = & \ \alpha \ln n_t + \beta \ln c_{y,t} + (1-\alpha-\beta)\ln c_{o,t+1} \\ & + \rho\big(\alpha \ln n_{t+1} + \beta \ln c_{y,t+1} + (1-\alpha-\beta)\ln c_{o,t+2}\big) \\ & + \cdots \\ & = \sum_{s=t}^{\infty} \rho^{s-t}\big(\alpha \ln n_s + \beta \ln c_{y,s} + (1-\alpha-\beta)\ln c_{o,s+1}\big). \end{aligned} \tag{57}$$

$0 < \rho < 1$ is assumed. The social welfare function is defined as the sum of the utilities of each generation, with each generation's utility weighted by ρ. Next, the resource constraint for period t is given as follows[10]:

$$Y_t = N_t c_{y,t} + N_t z n_t + N_{t-1} c_{o,t} + K_{t+1} \rightarrow k_t^{\theta} = c_{y,t} + z n_t + \frac{c_{o,t}}{n_{t-1}} + n_t k_{t+1}. \tag{58}$$

The socially desirable number of children and the allocation of consumption achieve the maximization of the social welfare function shown in (57), subject to the resource constraint in each period (58). The Lagrangian function is set as follows:

$$\begin{aligned} L = & \sum_{s=t}^{\infty} \rho^{s-t}\big(\alpha \ln n_s + \beta \ln c_{y,s} + (1-\alpha-\beta)\ln c_{o,s+1}\big) \\ & + \sum_{s=t}^{\infty} \lambda_s \left(k_s^{\theta} - c_{y,s} - z n_s - \frac{c_{o,s}}{n_{s-1}} - n_s k_{s+1}\right). \end{aligned} \tag{59}$$

The necessary condition of optimal allocations is shown as follows:

$$\frac{\partial L}{\partial n_t} = \frac{\alpha}{n_t} - \lambda_t (z + k_{t+1}) + \lambda_{t+1} \frac{c_{o,t+1}}{n_t^2} = 0, \tag{60}$$

$$\frac{\partial L}{\partial c_{y,t}} = \frac{\beta}{c_{y,t}} - \lambda_t = 0, \tag{61}$$

$$\frac{\partial L}{\partial c_{o,t+1}} = \frac{1-\alpha-\beta}{c_{o,t+1}} - \frac{\lambda_{t+1}}{n_t} = 0, \tag{62}$$

---

[9] Based on the work of van Groezen and Meijdam (2008), the social welfare function is defined. This social welfare function sums the utilities of each generation but does not weight them by population level. If weighting by population level were applied, the optimal number of children derived in this chapter would, of course, be derived differently.

[10] The left hand and the right hand denote the aggregate supply and the aggregate demand, respectively.

$$\frac{\partial L}{\partial k_{t+1}} = -\lambda_t n_t + \lambda_{t+1}\theta k_{t+1}^{\theta-1} = 0. \tag{63}$$

As shown by (20), (63) shows $\theta k_{t+1}^{\theta-1} = 1 + r_{t+1}$. Similarly, these can be derived for period $t + 1$. For example, (61) for period $t + 1$ is expressed as follows:

$$\frac{\partial L}{\partial c_{y,t+1}} = \frac{\rho\beta}{c_{y,t+1}} - \lambda_{t+1} = 0. \tag{64}$$

Considering (61), (63), (64), we can obtain the following equation:

$$\frac{\rho c_{y,t}}{c_{y,t+1}} = \frac{n_t}{1 + r_{t+1}}. \tag{65}$$

If we consider the steady state, because of $c_{y,t} = c_{y,t+1}$, the optimal number of children is shown as follows:

$$n = \rho(1 + r). \tag{66}$$

Because of (61)–(63), we obtain the following equation:

$$\frac{c_{o,t+1}}{c_{y,t}} = \frac{(1-\alpha-\beta)(1+r_{t+1})}{\beta}. \tag{67}$$

This equation is given by (12) and (13). In other words, the ratio of consumption in youth to consumption in old age aligns with the socially optimal level. By substituting (60)–(63) into (58), we can obtain the following equation[11]:

$$\frac{1}{\lambda_t} = \frac{\rho k_t^{\theta}}{\rho + 1 - \alpha - \beta} \tag{68}$$

By substituting (63) and (68) into (60) in the steady state, we can obtain the socially optimal level of capital stock by holding the following equation:

$$k = \frac{\theta(\rho + 1 - \alpha - \beta)z}{1 - \beta - \theta(\rho + 1 - \alpha - \beta)} \tag{69}$$

In general, the socially desirable number of children and the number of children chosen by households, derived in (21), do not match. Therefore, policies that change the number of children chosen by households through childcare support benefits are desirable. However, the number of children chosen by households is not always smaller than the socially desirable number of children. Conversely, under certain parameter conditions, it can be larger. In this case, to reduce the number of children, it would be desirable to implement policies that do the opposite of childcare support

[11] Regarding (62), when going back one period, consider $s = t - 1$, so note that $\frac{1-\alpha-\beta}{\rho c_{o,t}} = \frac{\lambda_t}{n_{t-1}}$.

benefits, such as collecting taxes based on the number of children to suppress the number of children.

Why is it that we cannot achieve a socially desirable allocation? This applies not only to capital stock but also to birth rates. The birth rate given in (66) is clearly different from that derived from an individual's optimization problem. One reason for this difference is the objective function. An individual's utility function includes only their own utility, whereas the social welfare function sums the utilities of individuals across various generations. Naturally, if the objective functions are different, the solutions will also differ. The second reason is externalities. The consumption and number of children chosen by individuals affect the overall capital stock of society, but individual optimization problems do not take this into account, leading to a discrepancy from the socially desirable allocation. This can be considered a problem of externalities. Although not discussed in this chapter, a pay-as-you-go pension system is directly influenced by the number of children, but individuals do not consider this effect on pension benefits when deciding the number of children. Whether this consideration is made or not clearly changes the number of children individuals decide to have. Details will be explained in chapter 3.

8 Conclusions

This chapter investigates how fertility rates are determined using basic endogenous fertility models, particularly within a two-period framework. It focuses on understanding the impact of childcare support policies on fertility rates.

The chapter employs simplified models to analyze the effects of childcare support policies in both open and closed economies. In closed economies, increased taxes for funding policies reduce household disposable income and savings, leading to lower corporate investments, decreased productivity, and ultimately fewer children. Conversely, in open economies, the ability to borrow from or invest in international markets helps mitigate these negative effects. The analysis demonstrates that the impact of childcare support policies varies depending on the economic context, suggesting that policies need to be tailored to specific economic conditions to effectively address declining birthrates.

Finally, it should be noted that there are various endogenous fertility models. Chen (2010) also sets up an endogenous fertility model in a two-period framework, which is the same as van Groezen and Meijdam (2008). They share the inclusion of survival probability in old age. However, Chen (2010) differs from van Groezen and Meijdam (2008) by considering educational investment. Nevertheless, it is evident that setting up an endogenous fertility model in a two-period framework is common in this field. Of course, there are also analyses in multi-period models. The most fundamental one is likely that of Barro and Becker (1989). In this model, the parent's utility function includes both the number of children and the children's utility function, set as an altruistic utility function, known as the dynasty model. About altruism, we should explore the model of Buchanan (1975). Parents decide the number of children and the allocation of consumption not only for the current period but also for future periods to maximize household utility. Although this model yields many implications, the fact that the dynasty model is more complex to handle compared to the two-period model might be the reason why two-period models have been increasing recently. In the case of the Ramsey model, there is also that of Petrucci (2015). Additionally, Yasuoka (2024) simulates the effects of childcare support policies within a Ramsey model using realistic parameters. This book mainly focuses on theoretical analysis, and by also reviewing papers with numerical analyses like these, we hope you will deepen your consideration of policy analysis in endogenous fertility models.

Appendix

A. Total Differentiation

In this book, the effects of policies are derived through total differentiation at various points. Here, we would like to explain total differentiation using (35) as an example. Below is (35) restated:

$$(z - q)n = \alpha(1 - \theta)k^{\theta}. \tag{35}$$

① Here, let's consider total differentiation with respect to q, n, and k. First, if $(z - q)n$ is differentiated by q, we obtain $-n$. This shows that it indicates how many units $-qn$ changes in an increase in a unit of q. If unit of dq increases, $-ndq$ increases.

② If $(z - q)n$ is differentiated by n, we obtain $z - q$. This shows that it indicates how many units $(z - q)n$ changes in an increase in a unit of n. If unit of dn changes, the change of $(z - q)n$ if given by $(z - q)dn$.

③ The total change in the left-hand side is $-ndq + (z - q)dn$.

④ If $\alpha(1 - \theta)k^{\theta}$ is differentiated by k, we obtain $\alpha\theta(1 - \theta)k^{\theta-1}$. This shows how many units $\alpha(1 - \theta)k^{\theta}$ changes in an increase in a unit of k. If unit of dk changes, the change of $\alpha(1 - \theta)k^{\theta}$ is $\alpha\theta(1 - \theta)k^{\theta-1}dk$.

⑤ Since the change in the left-hand side must equal the change in the right-hand side, the following equation holds:

$$-ndq + (z - q)dn = \alpha\theta(1 - \theta)k^{\theta-1}dk \rightarrow \frac{dn}{dq} = \frac{\alpha\theta(1 - \theta)k^{\theta-1}}{z - q}\frac{dk}{dq} + \frac{n}{z - q}. \tag{70}$$

Because of (24) and $\frac{dk}{dq}$, we obtain $\frac{dn}{dq}$. We want to see the effect of introducing childcare support benefits from a state where there were none, so we should substitute $q = 0$ into the derived $\frac{dn}{dq}$. This means differentiating at $q = 0$.

References

Barro, R. J., and Becker, G. S. (1989). Fertility choice in a model of economic growth. *Econometrica*, *57*(2), 481–501.

Buchanan, J. (1975). The samaritan's dilemma. In E. Phelps (Ed.), *Altruism, mortality and economic theory* (pp. 71–85). Russell Sage Foundation.

Chen, H.-J. (2010). Life expectancy, fertility, and educational investment. *Journal of Population Economics*, *23*(1), 37–56.

Oshio, T. (2001). Ikujishien・nenkinkaikaku to shusshoritsu [Child-care support, pension reform, and fertility]. *Kikan ShakaiHoshou Kenkyu* [*Quarterly of Social Security Research*], *36*(4), 535–546.

Petrucci, A. (2015). Optimal income taxation in models with endogenous fertility. *Journal of Macroeconomics*, *43*(C), 216–25.

van Groezen, B., Leers, T., and Meijdam, L. (2003). Social security and endogenous fertility: Pensions and child allowances as Siamese twins. *Journal of Public Economics*, *87*(2), 233–51.

van Groezen, B., and Meijdam, L. (2008). Growing old and staying young: Population policy in an ageing closed economy. *Journal of Population Economics*, *21*(3), 573–88.

Yasuoka, M. (2006). Shusshouritsu to kazeiseisaku no kankei [The relationship between fertility rate and tax policy]. *Kikan ShakaiHoshou Kenkyu* [*Quarterly of Social Security Research*], *42*(1), 80–90.

Yasuoka, M. (2007). Koteki ni kyoukyusareruikujizai wo dounyushitashusshouritsu naiseikamoderu ni okeru ikuji shien seisaku no kousatsu [A study of childcare support policy in the model based on endogenous fertility introduced the childcare goods provided publicly]. *Kikan ShakaiHoshou Kenkyu* [*Quarterly of Social Security Research*], *43*(3), 261–274.

Yasuoka M. (2024). Shusshouritsunaiseikamoderu ni okeru ikujishienseisaku no kouka no bunseki [Analysis of the effects of childcare policies in an endogenous fertility model]. *OIKONOMIKA*, *58*(2), 27–47.

Yasuoka, M., and Goto, N. (2011). Pension and child care policies with endogenous fertility. *Economic Modelling*, *28*, 2478–82.

Yasuoka, M., and Goto, N. (2015). How is the child allowance to be financed? By income tax or consumption tax? *International Review of Economics*, *62*(3), 249–69.

Data

Children and Families Agency, Government of Japan. (2024). *Sankou shiryou shu* [*Reference materials collection*]. https://www.cfa.go.jp/assets/contents/node/basic_page/field_ref_resources/b56819c6-3552-4be9-a55d-b29e69e32466/d0da3fff/20230402_policies_%E3%81%9F%E3%81%9F%E3%81%8D%E5%8F%B0_%E5%8F%82%E8%80%83%E8%B3%87%E6%96%99%EF%BC%88%E3%82%BB%E3%83%83%E3%83%88%E7%89%88%EF%BC%89.pdf

Ministry of Health, Labour, and Welfare of Japan. (2023). *Kousei roudou hakusho 2023* [*White paper on health, labour and welfare 2023*]. https://www.mhlw.go.jp/wp/hakusyo/kousei/22-2/kousei-data/pdfNFindex.html

Masaya Yasuoka is a professor at the School of Economics, Kwansei Gakuin University. His main areas of research interest are public finance, social security, and macroeconomics. He has published papers in scholarly journals including *Economics Letters*, *Economic Modelling*, *International Review of Economics* and *Journal of the Economics of Ageing*. Professor Yasuoka received a B.A. in economics from Nagoya City University and a Ph.D. in economics from Kobe University.

Chapter 2
Childcare Service and Fertility

Masaya Yasuoka

1 Introduction

The declining or rising trends in total fertility rates in advanced countries have been pointed out to be related to female labor force participation rates. Sleebos (2003) noted that in the 1980s, there was a negative correlation between female labor force participation rates and total fertility rates in OECD countries. On the other hand, in the 2000s, this correlation turned positive. The background to obtaining such a correlation is considered to be largely related to the opportunity cost of childcare. If women have to quit their jobs to give birth and raise children, they forgo the labor income they would have earned if they had continued working. This is the opportunity cost of childcare. As women's wage levels and female labor force participation rates increase, the existence of such opportunity costs becomes significant. The increase in these opportunity costs is explained as creating a declining trend in fertility rates.

However, on the other hand, it has been shown that in the 2000s, countries with higher female labor force participation rates also had higher total fertility rates. An important factor explaining this phenomenon is access to childcare services. By being able to access childcare services, working mothers can leave their children in daycare while they work, thus avoiding the need to quit their jobs for childcare. This eliminates the opportunity cost of childcare. Furthermore, as female labor force participation rates increase, household incomes rise, allowing families to allocate more resources to child-rearing. This increased financial capability may encourage having more children.

There are several prior studies that have modeled the relationship between female labor force participation rates and total fertility rates. One notable example is Galor and Weil (1996). Galor and Weil (1996) analyzed a setting in which a household consists of a male and a female, both of whom work to earn income, but the female

M. Yasuoka (✉)
School of Economics, Kwansei Gakuin University, Nishinomiya, Japan
e-mail: yasuoka@kwansei.ac.jp

M. Jinno and M. Yasuoka (eds.), *Fertility, Education and Macroeconomics: The Case of Japan*, https://doi.org/10.1007/978-981-95-1024-5_2

spends time on childcare. In this model, as female wage levels rise, the opportunity cost of childcare increases, leading to a reduction in the time allocated to childcare and consequently a decrease in fertility rates. This theoretical model aligns with the data showing a negative correlation between female labor force participation rates and total fertility rates.

Furthermore, Apps and Rees (2004) and Ferrero and Iza (2004) have presented theoretical models that align with data showing a positive correlation between female labor force participation rates and total fertility rates. Apps and Rees (2004) analyze a function where the number of children is determined by inputs of childcare services and women's childcare time. They argue that as female wage levels rise, the time women spend on childcare decreases, which could reduce the number of children. However, the increase in the purchase of childcare services results in an overall increase in the number of children. Ferrero and Iza (2004) consider capital accumulation in their model. They suggest that through capital accumulation, female wage levels rise, leading to the utilization of more affordable childcare services. This results in a positive relationship between female labor force participation rates and fertility rates.

Thus, in determining fertility rates, it is important to consider female labor force participation rates and childcare services. In this chapter, we will first present simplified models of Galor and Weil (1996) and Apps and Rees (2004), which take into account female labor force participation and childcare services. Following that, we will conduct an additional analysis that explicitly considers the childcare services market.

Figure 1 plots several OECD countries, but it does not necessarily show that countries with higher female labor participation rates also have higher birth rates. For example, France has a higher birth rate than Japan, despite having a lower female labor participation rate. This figure suggests that female labor participation rates alone cannot explain birth rates.

Figure 2 shows the trends in Japan's female labor participation rate, gender wage gap, and total fertility rate. Although the birth rate significantly dropped in 2005, overall, the data trends indicate a generally positive correlation.

The remainder of this chapter consists of the following. Section 2 and 3 explain the childcare time model and childcare services model, respectively. Section 4 shows the childcare services in two sectors model and Sect. 5 shows the childcare services and income inequality. The final section concludes this chapter.

2 Childcare Time Model

To begin, we will briefly explain the economic model set by Galor and Weil (1996) to analyze the relationship between female labor participation rates and birth rates. Galor and Weil (1996) consider an economic model where a household consists of a man and a woman. The man provides a fixed unit of labor and earns a wage w_m, while the woman divides one unit of her time between labor and childcare. Assuming

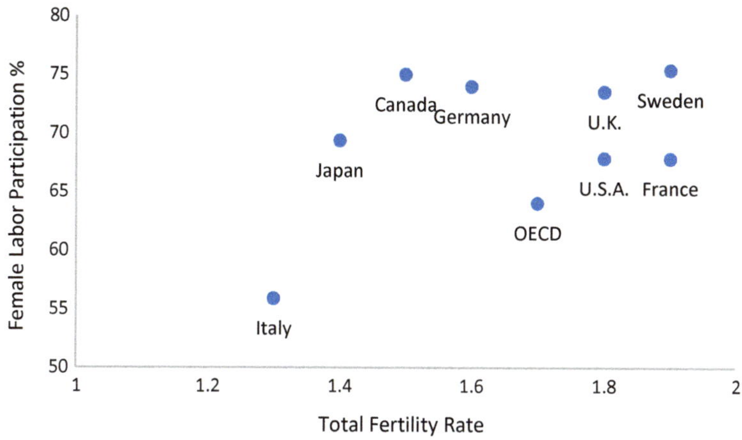

Fig. 1 Female labor participation and total fertility rate. *Source* OECD Statistics (2021). Female labor participation data is from 2017, and total fertility rate data is from 2016

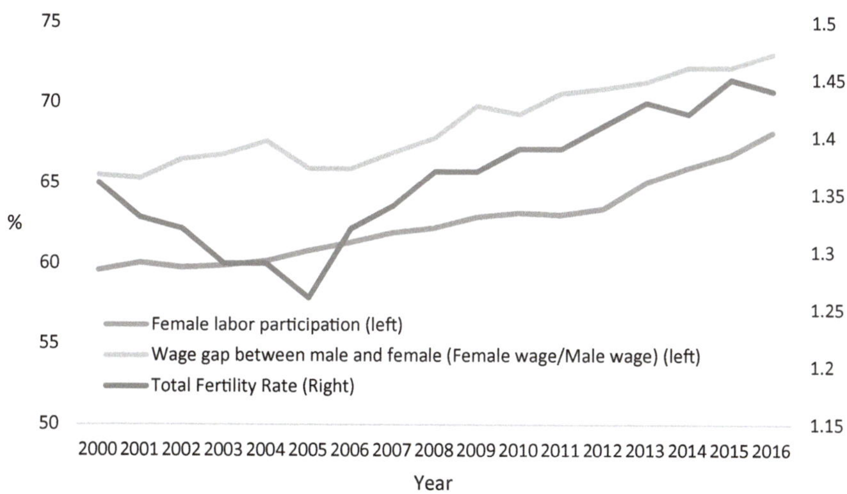

Fig. 2 Female labor participation, wage gap between male and female and total fertility rate in Japan. *Source* OECD Statistics (2021); The Japan Institute for Labour Policy and Training (2025)

that one child requires ϕ units of time, the woman's wage rate is w_f. If there are n children, the childcare time amounts to ϕn, and the woman's labor time becomes $1 - \phi n$. This labor time is considered the labor participation rate. Assuming the household allocates the total income earned to consumption c, the budget constraint can be expressed as follows:

$$\mathrm{c} = w_m + (1 - \phi n)w_f. \quad (1)$$

Assuming that utility is derived from consumption and the number of children, we postulate the following logarithmic utility function:

$$u = \alpha \ln n + (1 - \alpha) \ln c, 0 < \alpha < 1. \tag{2}$$

By solving the utility maximization problem, the number of children n is given as follows:

$$n = \frac{\alpha (w_m + w_f)}{\phi w_f} = \frac{\alpha}{\phi} \left(\frac{w_m}{w_f} + 1 \right). \tag{3}$$

What is shown here is that when the female labor wage rate increases, the number of children decreases. This is because the opportunity cost of childcare rises; in other words, the income lost due to the inability to work while providing childcare prompts individuals to reduce the number of children to decrease childcare time and increase labor time. This opportunity cost is considered the cost of childcare. The intuitive result derived by Galor and Weil (1996) is as described above. In practice, Galor and Weil (1996) consider capital accumulation, showing that over time, as the capital stock increases, the relative wages of female labor to male labor increase, the gender wage gap narrows, and the number of children decreases.

Such a result, where the cost of childcare leads to a reduction in the number of children, requires some adjustments in the setup. For example, if we consider a household as a single unit consisting of both a man and a woman, where the combined labor time is $1 - \phi n$, childcare time is ϕn, and the wage rate per unit time is w, the budget constraint in Eq. (1) can be modified as follows:

$$\mathrm{c} = (1 - \phi n) w. \tag{4}$$

Similarly, by solving the utility maximization problem, the number of children n will be a constant value as follows:

$$n = \frac{\alpha}{\phi}. \tag{5}$$

Regarding the result obtained in Eq. (5), it is a common outcome in the case of a logarithmic utility function. It is similar to the result in the labor-leisure choice model where leisure remains constant. Although income increases with rising wages, the cost of childcare also increases, so these effects exactly offset each other. The key point here is that while the cost of childcare rises with increasing wages, household income also increases simultaneously. In the formulation shown in Eq. (4), these two effects cancel each other out, resulting in no increase in the number of children.

If we consider income other than labor income, such as certain social security benefits, inheritance, or profits from owning a business, Eq. (4) can be modified as follows: Here, p represents income other than labor income.

$$c = (1 - \phi n)w + p \tag{6}$$

Similarly, by solving the utility maximization problem, the number of children n is given as follows:

$$n = \frac{\alpha(w + p)}{\phi w} = \frac{\alpha}{\phi}\left(\frac{p}{w} + 1\right). \tag{7}$$

In this way, it is shown that the number of children decreases with an increase in the wage rate. In this case, while the relationship indicates that the number of children decreases as the wage rate increases, if p increases (e.g., through higher social security benefits or increased financial assets), the number of children simultaneously increases. This can yield a positive relationship between (female) labor participation rates and birth rates.

However, Apps and Rees (2004) and Ferrero and Iza (2004) have shown that childcare services create a positive relationship between female labor participation rates and birth rates. In this chapter, we will also consider childcare services to explain the derivation of this relationship.

First, to modify the Galor and Weil (1996) model, the economic model we will consider assumes that both men and women allocate their entire unit of time to labor, and childcare is outsourced to childcare services. The cost of childcare services is assumed to be z per child. In this case, the budget constraint in Eq. (4) is modified as follows:

$$c + zn = w_m + w_f. \tag{8}$$

Then, the number of children is derived as follows:

$$n = \frac{\alpha\left(w_m + w_f\right)}{z}. \tag{9}$$

Here, it is shown that the number of children has a positive relationship with female wages. However, a strictly positive relationship between female labor participation rates and birth rates is not obtained here.

What should be noted is that while z is assumed to be constant over time and therefore increases with wages, z does not necessarily have to be constant. For example, if z is considered to be the cost of childcare services, when there is an increase in income and an attempt to increase the number of children, the demand for childcare services increases. Depending on the slope of the supply curve, the increased demand for childcare services may raise the price of these services, thereby restraining the use of childcare services and resulting in a smaller increase in the number of children. This outcome is demonstrated by Yasuoka and Miyake (2010).

3 Childcare Services Model

Here, we present a model in which an increase in female labor wages leads to an increase in female labor participation rates as well as birth rates. This model is set and analyzed by Apps and Rees (2004). We will present a simplified and more specific version of the model proposed by Apps and Rees (2004).

Consider a household with a man and a woman, where the man allocates all of his unit time to labor, while the woman allocates her unit time between childcare l and labor $1 - l$. The utility function of this household is given by Eq. (2). The budget constraint for this household is given as follows:

$$w_m + w_f(1 - l) = c + zx. \tag{10}$$

Here, w_m and w_f represent male and female wages, respectively; l is the childcare time; c is consumption; x is the childcare services; and z is the price of childcare services. Next, following Hirazawa and Yakita (2009), we assume the following birth rate function.

$$n = x^{\beta} l^{1-\beta}, 0 < \beta < 1. \tag{11}$$

The number of children n is determined by the input of childcare services x and childcare time l. Apps and Rees (2004) also assumed a birth rate function determined by the input of childcare services x and childcare time l,, defined as a homogenous function of degree one. This means that if both childcare services and childcare time are doubled, the number of children also doubles. Additionally, increasing childcare services leads to an increase in the number of children, but the incremental increase in the number of children diminishes. This is characterized by the property of diminishing marginal productivity (Fig. 3).[1]

When the input of childcare services is low, an increase in childcare services leads to a significant increase in the number of children. However, when a certain level of childcare service input is already being provided, additional input does not lead to a substantial increase in the number of children. The same can be said for childcare time.

Now, substituting the birth rate function (11) into the utility function (2), we obtain the following utility function:

$$u = \alpha\beta \ln x + \alpha(1 - \beta)\ln l + (1 - \alpha)\ln c. \tag{12}$$

---

[1] The function assumed by Hirazawa and Yakita (2009) is known as a Cobb–Douglas type function. On the other hand, the birth rate function defined by Kemnitz and Thum (2015) is a perfect substitutes linear function, such as $n = x + l$. Additionally, Kemnitz and Thum (2015) assume that men allocate a fixed unit of time to labor inelastically, while women allocate their unit of time between labor and childcare. Yasuoka (2014) assumes a CES type function, which relaxes the assumptions further compared to the Cobb–Douglas function.

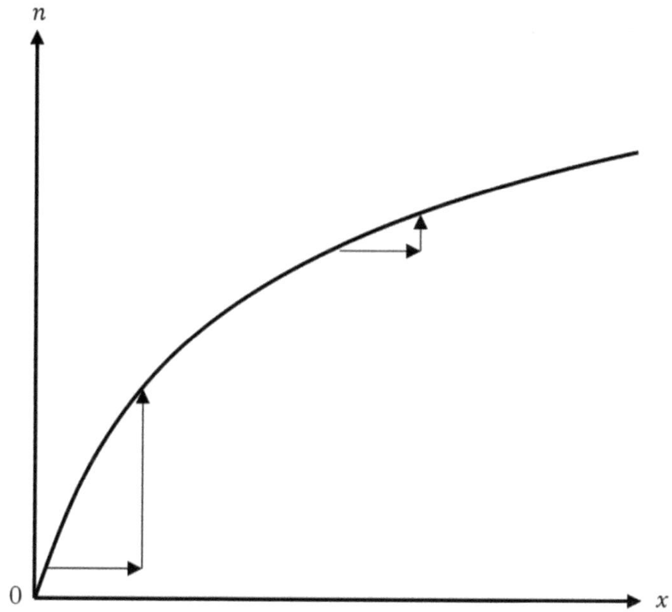

Fig. 3 Marginal productivity of childcare services

We consider the problem of maximizing the utility function (12) subject to the budget constraint (10). Childcare services x and childcare time l are given as follows:

$$x = \frac{\alpha\beta\left(w_m + w_f\right)}{z}, \tag{13}$$

$$l = \frac{\alpha(1-\beta)\left(w_m + w_f\right)}{w_f}. \tag{14}$$

By substituting (13) and (14) into (11), the number of children is obtained as follows:

$$n = \frac{\alpha\beta^{\beta}(1-\beta)^{1-\beta}\left(w_m + w_f\right)}{w_f^{1-\beta} z^{\beta}}. \tag{15}$$

Now, let's examine whether the number of children increases or decreases when the female labor wage w_f rises. Since w_f appears in both the numerator and the denominator, it is not immediately apparent what the overall impact will be. An increase in w_f raises household income, potentially increasing the purchase of childcare services and thus the number of children. On the other hand, it also raises the opportunity cost of childcare, which could reduce childcare time and thus decrease the number of children. Differentiating the number of children n, as shown in Eq. (15), with respect to the female labor wage w_f yields the following:

$$\frac{dn}{dw_f} = \left(\frac{1}{w_m + w_f} - \frac{1-\beta}{w_f}\right)n. \tag{16}$$

The condition of $\frac{dn}{dw_f} > 0$ is shown as follows:

$$\frac{w_m}{w_f} < \frac{\beta}{1-\beta}. \tag{17}$$

If the wage ratio between men and women falls below a certain level, it implies that the female labor wage is relatively high, and in this case, an increase in the female labor wage leads to an increase in the birth rate. As shown by Eqs. (13) and (14), an increase in the female labor wage w_f reduces childcare time l and increases childcare services x. The condition under which this increase is significant is given by inequality (17). Therefore, an increase in the female labor wage reduces childcare time and increases female labor supply. Considering labor supply as the labor participation rate, the condition in (17) indicates that a positive relationship between the female labor participation rate and the birth rate can be derived from the model.

Now, let's consider a subsidy for childcare services within this model. Suppose a lump-sum tax T is imposed on households and used as a subsidy for childcare services. In this case, the household budget constraint in Eq. (10) is modified as follows:

$$w_m + w_f(1-l) - T = c + (1-\gamma)zx, 0 < \gamma < 1. \tag{18}$$

γ denotes the subsidy rate. From the utility maximization problem, the demand for childcare services, the childcare time, and the number of children are given as follows:

$$x = \frac{\alpha\beta\left(w_m + w_f - T\right)}{(1-\gamma)z}, \tag{19}$$

$$l = \frac{\alpha(1-\beta)\left(w_m + w_f - T\right)}{w_f}, \tag{20}$$

$$n = \frac{\alpha\beta^\beta(1-\beta)^{1-\beta}\left(w_m + w_f - T\right)}{(1-\gamma)^\beta w_f^{1-\beta} z^\beta}. \tag{21}$$

Now, let's consider the government's budget constraint. Suppose there are N households, and a lump-sum tax T is imposed on each household. The revenue from this tax is used to provide a subsidy of γzx per household to N households. The government's budget constraint is then given by the following equation:

$$NT = N\gamma zx \rightarrow T = \gamma zx. \tag{22}$$

By substituting (22) into (21) and total differentiation of γ and n at $\gamma = 0$, we can obtain the following equation[2]:

$$\frac{dn}{d\gamma} = \beta(1 - \alpha)n > 0. \tag{23}$$

It is evident that a subsidy for childcare services increases the birth rate. Additionally, from Eq. (20), it can be seen that the increased tax burden for the subsidy reduces childcare time. Therefore, the fact that the birth rate is increasing while childcare time is decreasing indicates that the demand for childcare services is correspondingly increasing.

So far, our analysis has considered the price of childcare services as fixed. In reality, the price of childcare services is determined by the extent of demand and supply for these services. To understand the demand and supply of childcare services, it is necessary to consider the childcare services sector as a production sector. In the next section, we will explore a two-sector model that takes childcare services into account.

4 Market of Childcare Services in Two Sectors Model

Here, let's consider an economic model where consumer goods and childcare services are produced in separate markets. First, for the sector producing consumer goods, individuals engaged in this sector receive wages w_m for male labor and w_f for female labor. The price of consumer goods is normalized to 1.

On the other hand, in the sector producing childcare services, individuals engaged in this sector receive a wage w_f for female labor. In fact, since many childcare workers in Japan are women, it is realistic to assume that the female labor wage w_f is received in the childcare market. Women are free to choose whether to work in the consumer goods production sector or the childcare services production sector, and the wage rates are equalized between the two sectors. If the wage in one sector is higher than in the other, labor will move to the higher-paying sector. This shift causes the wages in the relatively understaffed sector to rise, thereby equalizing wages.

Now, let's assume the production function X_t for the childcare services sector is as follows:

[2] If (21) is shown by the logarithm form, $\ln n = \ln\alpha\beta^{\beta}(1-\beta)^{1-\beta} + \ln(w_m + w_f - \gamma zx) - (1-\beta)\ln w_f - \beta\ln(1-\gamma) - \beta\ln z$ is shown. Total differentiation of γ and n at $\gamma = 0$ derives $\frac{dn}{n} = -\frac{zxd\gamma}{w_m+w_f} + \beta d\gamma$ and we obtain (23). In $\gamma = 0$, $zx = \alpha\beta(w_m + w_f)$. By differentiation of $\gamma = 0$, for instance, (22) is shown by $dT = zxd\gamma + \gamma xdz + \gamma zdx$. However, by considering $\gamma = 0$, we obtain $dT = zxd\gamma$. This can be considered the effect of introducing a subsidy for childcare services. By performing such calculations, it is easier to obtain a definitive sign.

$$X_t = \rho L_t^c, 0 < \rho. \tag{24}$$

Here, L_t^c denotes the number of workers in the childcare services sector, ρ is a parameter indicating productivity, and t represents time. Such a linear function in the childcare services sector has been assumed by Yasuoka and Miyake (2010), and a similar linear function for the caregiving services sector has been considered by Hashimoto and Tabata (2010). Next, the profit function is given as follow:

$$\pi_t = z_t \rho L_t^c - w_t^c L_t^c. \tag{25}$$

Because of profit maximization, we obtain $z_t = \frac{w_t^c}{\rho}$. Because of $w_t^c = w_f$, we obtain

$$z = \frac{w_f}{\rho}, \tag{26}$$

and the price of childcare services is constant over time. In other words, if the wage rate in the consumer goods sector does not change, the wage rate in the childcare services sector also does not change, and therefore the price of childcare services remains unchanged. However, this result assumes that childcare services are produced using a linear technology, meaning that the additional amount of childcare services produced by increasing labor by one unit is constant regardless of the production level of childcare services. In other words, it assumes that the marginal productivity of labor does not diminish.

Now, let's modify this assumption slightly. Assume the production function for childcare services is as follows:

$$X_t = \rho L_t^{c\theta}, 0 < \rho, 0 < \theta < 1. \tag{27}$$

With such a production function, as illustrated in the following figure, the marginal productivity of labor diminishes (Fig. 4).

The profit function can be set as follows:

$$\pi_t = z_t \rho L_t^{c\theta} - w_t^c L_t^c. \tag{28}$$

In this case, unlike Eq. (25), the profit does not become zero. The profit is illustrated in the following figure. It is given by the difference between the revenue from childcare services and the cost of producing these services.

The length of the arrow between the curve and the line represents the profit. This profit varies with the amount of labor input. For instance, in Fig. 5, there are three arrows, and the middle arrow is the longest, indicating that the profit is highest at that point. The number of workers that maximizes this profit can be determined by calculating, $\frac{d\pi_t}{dL_t^c} = 0$. The calculation is as follows:

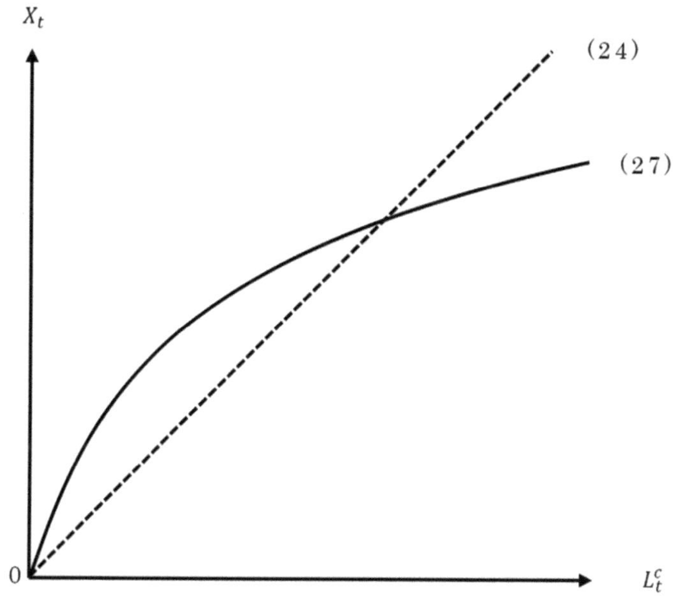

Fig. 4 Marginal productivity of childcare services

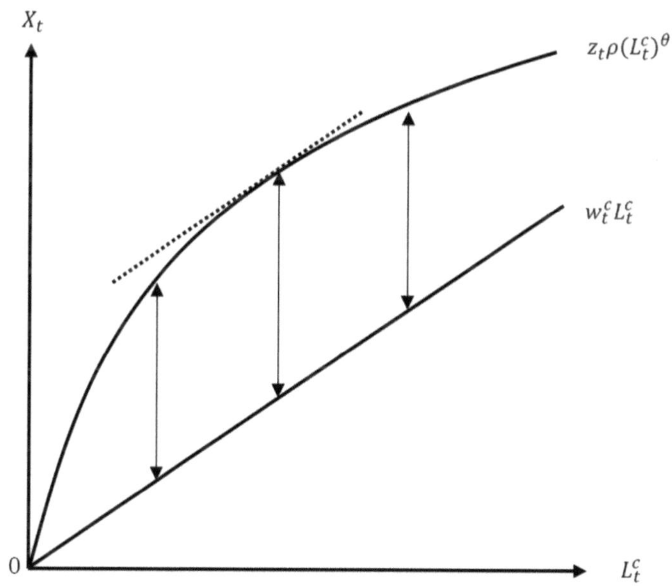

Fig. 5 Marginal productivity of childcare services

$$\frac{d\pi_t}{dL_t^c} = \theta z_t \rho L_t^{c\theta-1} - w_t^c = 0 \rightarrow \frac{w_t^c}{z_t} = \theta\rho L_t^{c\theta-1}. \tag{29}$$

The left-hand side of Eq. (29) represents the real wage, and the right-hand side represents the marginal productivity of labor. The condition for profit maximization is that these two are equal. Since the wage rate for female labor is given by the consumer goods market, and assuming women can freely choose to work in either sector, the wages will be equalized through intersectoral mobility. Therefore, we obtain the following equation:

$$\frac{w_f}{z_t} = \theta\rho L_t^{c\theta-1}. \tag{30}$$

Furthermore, using the production function (27), the supply function of childcare services, which shows the relationship between z_t and X_t, can be expressed as follows:

$$z_t = \frac{w_f}{\theta\rho^{\frac{1}{\theta}}} X_t^{\frac{1-\theta}{\theta}}. \tag{31}$$

The demand for childcare services is given by Eq. (13), and the supply is given by Eq. (31).[3] The equilibrium level of childcare services, where demand equals supply, can be expressed as $X_t = x_t$ and is given as follows[4]:

$$x_t = \rho\left(\alpha\beta\theta\left(\frac{w_m}{w_f} + 1\right)\right)^{\theta}. \tag{32}$$

The demand curve and supply curve are illustrated as follows, with the intersection of both curves representing the equilibrium quantity and equilibrium price of childcare services as indicated in Eq. (32).

Now, let's explain the effects of a subsidy policy for childcare services using Fig. 6. Suppose the funding for the subsidy is collected through a lump-sum tax, and the subsidy rate for childcare services is γ. The demand function, then, is given as follows, in the same form as Eq. (19):

$$x_t = \frac{\alpha\beta\left(w_m + w_f - T\right)}{(1-\gamma)z_t}. \tag{33}$$

Then, we can show the following Fig. 7:

[3] In the case of the production function for the childcare services sector, profits are generated. If households receive these profits, it would influence the household's demand for childcare services through the addition of a profit term to the budget constraint. Although including this effect in the analysis might not fundamentally change the conclusions of this chapter, it would complicate the analysis. Therefore, for simplicity, we proceed without incorporating the profits into the analysis.

[4] We normalize the size of firms and households to one, respectively.

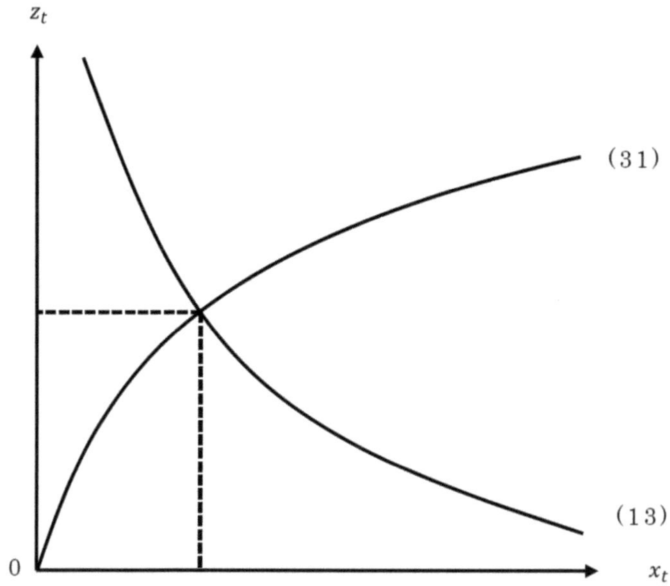

Fig. 6 Quantity and price of childcare services at equilibrium (for instance, the supply curve is the case of $\theta > \frac{1}{2}$)

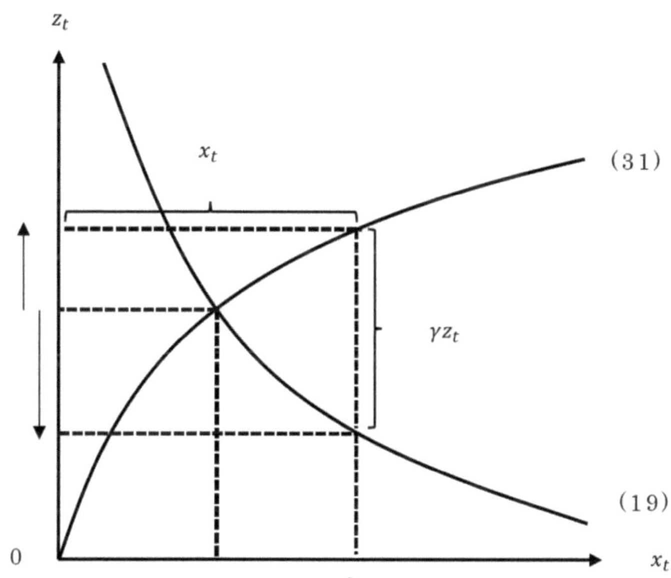

Fig. 7 Effect of subsidy policy for childcare service

Figure 7 illustrates an ad valorem subsidy where a subsidy of γz_t per unit of childcare services results in a demand quantity of x_t units. The total subsidy amount is represented by the area of the rectangle with a vertical length of γz_t and a horizontal length of x_t. Due to the subsidy, the demand increases by the length of the horizontal arrow. This is because the subsidy policy reduces the price available to households (referred to as the consumer price) by the length of the downward arrow on the vertical axis, thereby promoting utilization. On the other hand, the price that firms receive for providing one unit of childcare services (referred to as the producer price) increases by the length of the upward arrow on the vertical axis due to the subsidy policy, thereby promoting supply.

Now, let's examine the effects of this subsidy in mathematical terms. First, by totally differentiating Eq. (31) with respect to z_t and x_t, we obtain the following equation:

$$\frac{dz_t}{dx_t} = \frac{w_f(1-\theta)}{\theta^2\rho^{\frac{1}{\theta}}} x_t^{\frac{1}{\theta}-2}. \tag{34}$$

By totally differentiating Eq. (22) with respect to T and γ at $\gamma = 0$, we obtain the following equation:

$$dT = z_t x_t \gamma. \tag{35}$$

By totally differentiation Eq. (33) with respect to T, γ, x_t and z_t at $\gamma = 0$, we obtain the following equation:

$$-z_t x_t d\gamma + x_t dz_t + z_t dx_t = -\alpha\beta dT. \tag{36}$$

By substituting (34) and (35) into (36), the subsidy policy can increase the equilibrium quantity of childcare services:

$$\frac{dx_t}{d\gamma} = \frac{(1-\alpha\beta)z_t x_t}{z_t + \frac{w_f(1-\theta)}{\theta^2\rho^{\frac{1}{\theta}}} x_t^{\frac{1}{\theta}-1}} > 0. \tag{37}$$

However, due to the funding obtained through a lump-sum tax, the amount of childcare time decreases. While the provision of childcare services increases, the reduction in childcare time means that the number of children does not necessarily increase.

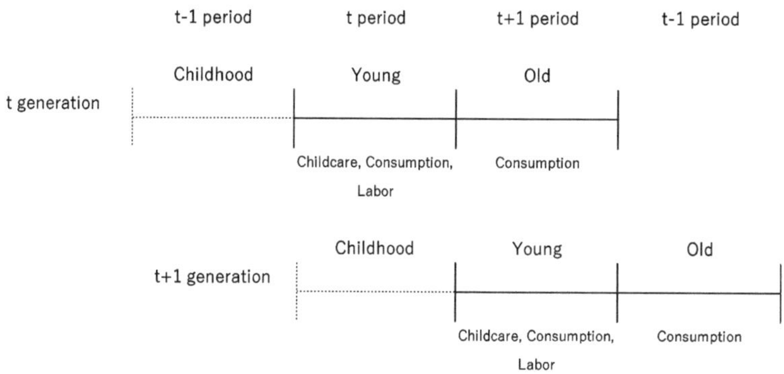

Fig. 8 The behavior of each generation[6]

5 Income Inequality and Childcare Services

Shintani and Yasuoka (2022) consider two sectors: the sector producing goods such as consumer goods (referred to as the final goods production sector) and the sector producing childcare services. They examine how childcare support policies and aging affect not only the birth rate and per capita capital stock but also the wage gap between the two sectors. Below, we will outline the model and examine the effects of childcare support policies.[5]

First, the utility function of the household is assumed to be as follows:

$$u = \alpha \ln n_t + \beta \ln c_{y,t} + (1 - \alpha - \beta) \ln c_{o,t+1}, \quad 0 < \alpha < 1, \quad 0 < \beta < 1, \quad \alpha + \beta < 1. \tag{38}$$

Here, n_t is the number of children, $c_{y,t}$ is consumption during the young period, and $c_{o,t+1}$ is consumption during the old period. An individual in this household lives through two periods, young and old. In the first period, the young period, the individual supplies one unit of labor inelastically, earning labor income. This income is allocated to childcare costs, consumption during the young period, and savings for consumption during the old period. In the second period, the old period, the individual receives the principal and interest from the savings, which are used for consumption during the old period. The structure of each generation is as follows (Fig. 8).

Furthermore, it is assumed that a certain training cost is required to work in the final goods sector. This training cost varies among individuals and is assumed to be uniformly distributed in the range $[0, \bar{\sigma}]$. This setting follows the model proposed

[5] Shintani and Yasuoka (2022) present a macroeconomic model that considers money holdings, but here we provide a simplified version of the model that abstracts from the monetary sector.

[6] It should be noted that individuals live through three periods including childhood, but since no decisions are made during childhood, it is essentially a two-period model.

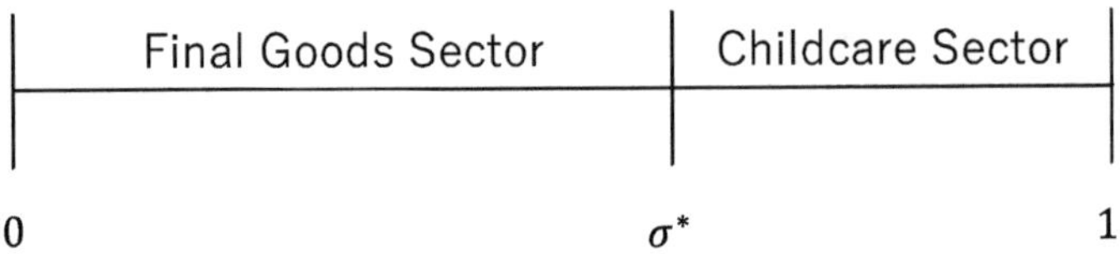

Fig. 9 The labor share of each sector

by Caselli (1999).[7] In other words, some individuals incur very little training cost, while others incur a high training cost, with each level of training cost being equally likely within the specified range.[8]

The income earned from working in the final goods sector is the wage w minus the training cost σ, resulting in $w - \sigma$. On the other hand, let the wage in the childcare services sector be w^c. The training cost σ^* of the individual who is indifferent between working in the final goods sector and the childcare services sector is determined by the following equation:

$$w - \sigma^* = w^c. \tag{39}$$

Individuals with training costs $\sigma < \sigma^*$ will work in the final goods sector, while those with $\sigma > \sigma^*$ will work in the childcare services sector.

Now, consider that all individuals live under one roof and form a single household. In this household, there are both individuals working in the final goods sector and individuals working in the childcare services sector. Given that $\bar{\sigma}=1$, the proportions of workers in each sector are σ^* for the final goods sector and $1-\sigma^*$ for the childcare services sector (Fig. 9).

Now, let's explain the budget constraint. The budget constraint during the young period is as follows:

$$z_t n_t + c_{y,t} + s_t = \int_0^{\sigma_t^*} (w_t - \sigma_t) d\sigma_t + \left(1 - \sigma_t^*\right) w_t^c. \tag{40}$$

z_t represents the cost of childcare services. The budget constraint during the old period is as follows:

$$(1 + r_{t+1}) s_t = c_{o,t+1}. \tag{41}$$

[7] Meckl and Zink (2004) present an economic model where, instead of training costs, the wage levels received in each sector vary by individual. This variation determines the proportion of workers in each sector.

[8] Here, we are considering a uniform distribution for the distribution function, but it can also be considered using a normal distribution. While a normal distribution is more realistic as the proportion decreases the further it is from the mean, to keep the solutions derived from the model simple, we assume a uniform distribution. It is believed that the essential results would not change even with a uniform distribution.

Here, r_{t+1} is the interest rate. Combining the constraints, the lifetime budget constraint is as follows:

$$z_t n_t + c_{y,t} + \frac{c_{o,t+1}}{1 + r_{t+1}} = \int_0^{\sigma_t^*} (w_t - \sigma_t) d\sigma_t + \left(1 - \sigma_t^*\right) w_t^c. \tag{42}$$

Under budget constraint (42), the allocation that maximizes utility function (38) can be determined by solving the utility maximization problem. As a result, the number of children and savings are derived as follows:

$$n_t = \frac{\alpha\left(\int_0^{\sigma_t^*} (w_t - \sigma_t) d\sigma_t + \left(1 - \sigma_t^*\right) w_t^c\right)}{z_t}, \tag{43}$$

$$s_t = (1 - \alpha - \beta)\left(\int_0^{\sigma_t^*} (w_t - \sigma_t) d\sigma_t + \left(1 - \sigma_t^*\right) w_t^c\right). \tag{44}$$

Additionally, let the production function of the final goods sector be $Y_t = K_t^\theta L_t^{1-\theta}$ where $0 < \theta < 1$. Here, Y_t is the output of the final goods, K_t is the capital stock, and L_t is the labor input. Considering profit-maximizing behavior in a perfectly competitive market, the wage rate and interest rate are given as follows:

$$w_t = (1 - \theta) k_t^\theta, \tag{45}$$

$$1 + r_t = \theta k_t^{\theta - 1}. \tag{46}$$

$k_t = \frac{K_t}{L_t} = \frac{K_t}{\sigma^* N_t}$ represents the capital stock per worker in the final goods sector. Here, N_t is the population size of the young generation in period t. Furthermore, it is assumed that capital accumulation depreciates over one period. So, what would be the dynamic equation for this capital stock k? The equilibrium equation for the capital market is given by $K_{t+1} = N_t s_t$, which represents the total savings in period t, which is equal to the investment in period t. Further, the investments made in period t contribute to production as capital stock in period $t + 1$. Thus, for $K_{t+1} = N_t s_t$, $k_t = \frac{K_t}{L_t} = \frac{K_t}{\sigma_t^* N_t}$, from (39) and (43), the dynamic equation for k_t can be expressed as follows[9]:

$$n_t \sigma_{t+1}^* k_{t+1} = (1 - \alpha - \beta)\left(\int_0^{\sigma_t^*} (w_t - \sigma_t) d\sigma_t + \left(1 - \sigma_t^*\right)\left(w_t - \sigma_t^*\right)\right). \tag{47}$$

Let the production function of the childcare sector be $Y_t^c = \rho L_t^c$. Here, Y_t^c represents the output of childcare services, L_t^c is the labor input in childcare services, and ρ is a positive parameter. From the profit maximization condition, $w_t^c = z_t \rho$. The price of childcare services can be expressed using Eq. (39) as follows:

---

[9] We notify that $\frac{K_{t+1}}{L_{t+1}} \frac{L_{t+1}}{N_{t+1}} \frac{N_{t+1}}{N_t} N_t = n_t \sigma_{t+1}^* k_{t+1} N_t$ can be derived.

$$z_t = \frac{w_t - \sigma_t^*}{\rho}. \tag{48}$$

From Eqs. (43) and (48), the proportion of workers engaged in childcare services can be expressed as follows:

$$\frac{\alpha\left(\int_0^{\sigma_t^*}(w_t - \sigma_t)d\sigma_t + \left(1 - \sigma_t^*\right)\left(w_t - \sigma_t^*\right)\right)}{z_t} = \rho\left(1 - \sigma_t^*\right). \tag{49}$$

σ_t^* is determined such that the left-hand side and right-hand side of Eq. (49) are equal, and as a result, the proportion of workers engaged in childcare services is determined. Then, the birth rate is expressed as follows:

$$n_t = \frac{\alpha\left(\int_0^{\sigma_t^*}(w_t - \sigma_t)d\sigma_t + \left(1 - \sigma_t^*\right)\left(w_t - \sigma_t^*\right)\right)}{z_t} = \rho\left(1 - \sigma_t^*\right). \tag{50}$$

Thus, the birth rate is determined by the number of workers engaged in childcare services. So, what happens to the number of workers engaged in childcare services as the capital stock increases? With an increase in capital stock, the wage rate in the final goods sector increases, leading workers with high training costs to seek employment in the final goods sector, which may reduce the number of workers in the childcare services sector. However, considering Eq. (39), the wage rate in the childcare services sector will also increase, and considering Eq. (50), the demand for childcare services will rise with the increase in the wage rate in the final goods sector. As a result, the price of childcare services will increase, leading to a rise in the wage rate in the childcare services sector.

Let us derive the dynamic equation for capital stock by substituting Eqs. (45), (48), and (50) into Eq. (47). The equation is expressed as follows:

$$\begin{aligned} k_{t+1} &= \frac{(1 - \alpha - \beta)\left(\int_0^{\sigma_t^*}(w_t - \sigma_t)d\sigma_t + \left(1 - \sigma_t^*\right)\left(w_t - \sigma_t^*\right)\right)}{n_t \sigma_{t+1}^*} \\ &= \frac{(1 - \alpha - \beta)\left(w_t - \sigma_t^*\right)}{\rho\alpha\sigma_{t+1}^*}. \end{aligned} \tag{51}$$

k_t, σ_t^* is determined from Eq. (49). Consider that σ_{t+1}^* is a function of k_{t+1}, k_{t+1} determined by Eq. (51), and the capital stock for each period is derived. Consequently, endogenous variables for each period, such as the consumption level and the proportion of workers in childcare services, are also determined.[10] Furthermore, the wage gap between the two sectors can be expressed as follows:

[10] By substituting $k_{t+1} = k_t = k$ into (51), the steady-state capital stock can be determined. Additionally, the stability condition can be obtained by finding $\frac{dk_{t+1}}{dk_t}$ and substituting the steady-state capital stock.

$$\frac{w_t^c}{w_t} = \frac{w_t - \sigma_t^*}{w_t} = 1 - \frac{\sigma_t^*}{w_t}. \tag{52}$$

If the capital stock continues to increase and the wage rate in the final goods sector continues to rise, the wage of the childcare services sector relative to the wage in the final goods sector will become progressively smaller, leading to a widening gap. However, if σ_t^* rises along with the increase in capital stock, the gap does not necessarily widen.

Next, we would like to consider a case where a subsidy is provided for the demand for childcare services as a childcare support policy. Specifically, a subsidy q_t is given to households for each child. The source of this subsidy is financed by collecting labor income tax from the young generation. In this case, the household's lifetime budget constraint is modified as follows:

$$(z_t - q_t)n_t + c_{y,t} + \frac{c_{o,t+1}}{1+r_{t+1}} = (1-\tau)\left(\int_0^{\sigma_t^*} (w_t - \sigma_t)d\sigma_t + \left(1-\sigma_t^*\right)\left(w_t - \sigma_t^*\right)\right). \tag{53}$$

By solving the utility maximization problem, the number of children and savings can be expressed as follows:

$$n_t = \frac{\alpha(1-\tau)\left(\int_0^{\sigma_t^*} (w_t - \sigma_t)d\sigma_t + \left(1-\sigma_t^*\right)\left(w_t - \sigma_t^*\right)\right)}{z_t - q_t}, \tag{54}$$

$$s_t = (1-\alpha-\beta)(1-\tau)\left(\int_0^{\sigma_t^*} (w_t - \sigma_t)d\sigma_t + \left(1-\sigma_t^*\right)\left(w_t - \sigma_t^*\right)\right). \tag{55}$$

At this time, if the tax rate is denoted by τ, the government's budget constraint can be expressed as follows:

$$q_t n_t = \tau\left(\int_0^{\sigma_t^*} (w_t - \sigma_t)d\sigma_t + \left(1-\sigma_t^*\right)\left(w_t - \sigma_t^*\right)\right)$$
$$\rightarrow q_t = \frac{\tau\left(\int_0^{\sigma_t^*} (w_t - \sigma_t)d\sigma_t + \left(1-\sigma_t^*\right)\left(w_t - \sigma_t^*\right)\right)}{n_t}. \tag{56}$$

In the steady state, the capital stock, birth rate, and the proportion of workers engaged in childcare services can be expressed as follows:

$$k = \frac{(1-\alpha-\beta)(1-\tau)\left(\int_0^{\sigma^*} (w - \sigma)d\sigma + (1-\sigma^*)(w-\sigma^*)\right)}{n\sigma^*}, \tag{57}$$

$$n = \frac{\alpha(1-\tau)\left(\int_0^{\sigma^*} (w - \sigma)d\sigma + (1-\sigma^*)(w-\sigma^*)\right)}{z - q}, \tag{58}$$

$$\frac{\alpha(1-\tau)\left(\int_0^{\sigma^*}(w-\sigma)d\sigma_t+(1-\sigma^*)(w-\sigma^*)\right)}{z-q}=\rho\left(1-\sigma^*\right). \tag{59}$$

Here, $w = (1-\theta)k^{\theta}$ and $z = \frac{w-\sigma^*}{\rho}$. Equation (57) is the dynamic equation for capital, Eq. (58) represents the birth rate, and Eq. (59) determines the number of workers in the childcare services sector.

Let's intuitively grasp the effects of the policy from these equations. First, from Eq. (58), if the childcare support benefit q increases, the denominator decreases, leading to an increase in the birth rate n. If the birth rate n increases, then from Eq. (57), σ^* decreases, resulting in an increase in the proportion of workers engaged in the childcare services sector. On the other hand, regarding the capital stock k, since the tax rate τ is included in the numerator of Eq. (57), it reduces the capital stock. However, since σ^* is included in both the numerator and the denominator, it increases the capital stock. Further, the increase in the birth rate n leads to a decrease in the capital stock. Therefore, it is unclear whether the capital stock will increase or decrease. The impact on the wage gap between sectors, shown in Eq. (52), also remains uncertain. If the capital stock decreases due to the policy, the childcare support policy will increase the proportion of workers engaged in childcare services and reduce the wage gap with the final goods sector.

Figure 10 presents actual data. Over the past decade, there has been an upward trend in the total fertility rate, and correspondingly, the number of workers in the childcare services market has also increased. Additionally, the level of childcare support policies has risen. These changes are consistent with the analysis presented so far. However, regarding the wage gap, while there are periods of increase over a few years, it has been relatively flat over the ten-year period. This suggests that there are various factors at play, such as economic fluctuations, which cannot be explained by this model alone.

6 Conclusion

Sleebos (2003) demonstrated that the correlation between female labor participation rates and fertility rates in developed countries has shifted from negative to positive. A similar empirical study by Ahn and Mira (2002) also shows that this correlation has turned positive in developed countries. The policy implication of these findings is that policies enabling the compatibility of childcare and work are desirable. It is essential to avoid the significant opportunity costs associated with leaving the workforce. Childcare services are a key point in achieving this.

In this chapter, childcare services refer to those provided in the market, such as daycare centers and babysitters. Of course, instead of using market-provided childcare services, grandparents can also be considered as caregivers from the child's

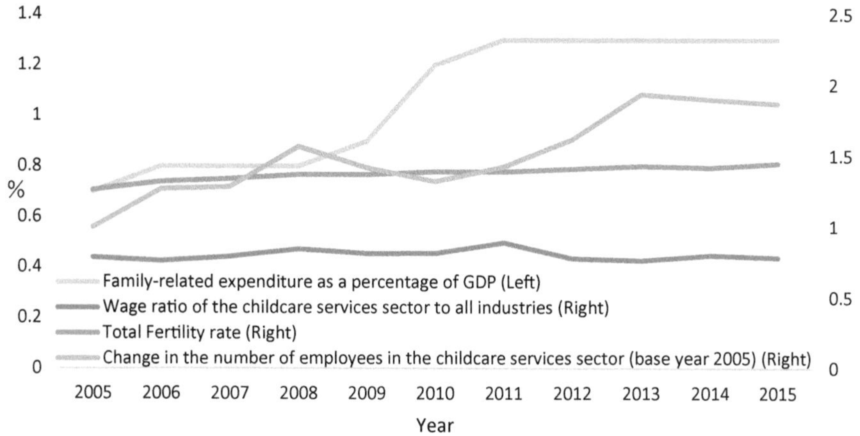

Fig. 10 Number of workers in the childcare services market, wage level, birth rate, family-related social expenditure. *Source* Ministry of Health, Labour and Welfare (2021)

perspective. Although this chapter does not cover this aspect, further details can be found in Yasuoka, Azetsu, and Akiyama (2009).

Regarding the division of childcare between genders, this chapter takes a very simple approach. In reality, various models, such as bargaining models between spouses, can be considered. For instance, Oguro and Yasuoka (2017) clarified how fertility rates are determined under the assumption of equal bargaining power between spouses. Previous studies on bargaining between spouses include that of Konrad and Lommerud (2000). While several endogenous fertility models considering spousal bargaining power already exist, this chapter limits itself to introducing the literature due to space constraints.

Appendix

A. Household's Optimal Allocations (13), (14)

We set the following Lagrange function L.

$$L = \alpha\beta \ln x + \alpha(1-\beta)\ln l + (1-\alpha)\ln c + \lambda\left(w_m + w_f(1-l) - c - zx\right) \tag{60}$$

The necessary condition of optimal allocations are shown as follows:

$$\frac{\partial L}{\partial x} = \frac{\alpha\beta}{x} - \lambda z = 0 \rightarrow \frac{\alpha\beta}{\lambda} = zx, \tag{61}$$

$$\frac{\partial L}{\partial l} = \frac{\alpha(1-\beta)}{l} - \lambda w_f = 0 \rightarrow \frac{\alpha(1-\beta)}{\lambda} = l w_f, \tag{62}$$

$$\frac{\partial L}{\partial c} = \frac{1-\alpha}{c} - \lambda = 0 \rightarrow \frac{1-\alpha}{\lambda} = c, \tag{63}$$

$$\frac{\partial L}{\partial \lambda} = w_m + w_f(1-l) - c - zx = 0. \tag{64}$$

By considering (61)–(63), we can obtain the following:

$$\frac{1}{\lambda} = w_m + w_f. \tag{65}$$

Therefore, by considering (61), (62) and (65), we obtain (14).

References

Ahn, N., & Mira, P. (2002). A note on the changing relationship between fertility and female employment rates in developed countries. *Journal of Population Economics, 15*(4), 667–82.

Apps, P., and Rees, R. (2004). Fertility, taxation and family policy. *Scandinavian Journal of Economics, 106*(4), 745–63.

Caselli, F. (1999). Technological revolutions. *American Economic Review, 89*(1), 78–102.

Ferrero, M. D., and Iza, A. (2004). Skill premium effects on fertility and female labor force supply. *Journal of Population Economics, 17*(1), 1–16.

Galor O., and Weil D. N. (1996). The gender gap, fertility, and growth. *American Economic Review, 86*(3), 374–87.

Hashimoto, K., and Tabata, K. (2010). Population aging, health care, and growth. *Journal of Population Economics, 23*(2), 571–93.

Hirazawa, M., and Yakita, A. (2009). Fertility, child care outside the home, and pay-as-you-go social security. *Journal of Population Economics, 22*(3), 565–83.

Kemnitz, A., and Thum, M. (2015). Gender power, fertility, and family policy. *Scandinavian Journal of Economics, 117*(1), 220–47.

Konrad, K. A., and Lommerud, K. E. (2000). The bargaining family revisited. *Canadian Journal of Economics, 33*(2), 471–87.

Meckl, J., and Zink, S. (2004). Solow and heterogeneous labour: A neoclassical explanation of wage inequality. *Economic Journal, 114*(498), 825–43.

Oguro, K., and Yasuoka, M. (2017). *Stress, child care, and fertility*. Discussion paper Series 153, School of Economics, Kwansei Gakuin University.

Shintani, M., and Yasuoka, M. (2022). Fertility, inequality and income growth. *Italian Economic Journal, 8*(1), 29–48.

Sleebos, J. (2003). *Low fertility rates in OECD countries: Facts and policy responses*. OECD Labour Market and Social Policy Occasional Papers 15, OECD Publishing.

Yasuoka, M. (2014). *Child-care policies and pension in an endogenous fertility model*. Discussion Paper Series 114, School of Economics, Kwansei Gakuin University.

Yasuoka, M., Azetsu, K., and Akiyama, T. (2009). Intergenerational child care support and the fluctuating fertility: A note. *Economics Bulletin, 29*(4), 2478–91.

Yasuoka, M., and Miyake, A. (2010). Change in the transition of the fertility rate. *Economics Letters, 106*(2), 78–80.

Data

Cabinet Office, Government of Japan. (2021). *Shoushikashakaitaisakuhakusho 2018* [*White paper on measures to cope with a declining birthrate society 2018*]. https://warp.da.ndl.go.jp/info:ndljp/pid/12772297/www8.cao.go.jp/shoushi/shoushika/whitepaper/measures/w-2018/30webhonpen/index.html

Ministry of Health, Labour and Welfare. (2021). *Chinginkouzoukihonchousa* [*Basic survey on wage structure*]. https://www.mhlw.go.jp/toukei/list/chinginkouzou.html

Ministry of Health, Labour and Welfare. (2024). *Jinkoudoutaitoukei* [*Demographic survey*]. https://www.mhlw.go.jp/toukei/list/81-1a.html

OECD Statistics. (2021). https://stats.oecd.org/

The Japan Institute for Labour Policy and Training. (2025). *Hayawakari: Gurafu de miru zu 6-danjokanchinginkakusa* [*Quick understanding: Long-term labor statistics in graphs, Figure 6: Wage gap between men and women*]. https://www.jil.go.jp/kokunai/statistics/timeseries/html/g0406.html

Masaya Yasuoka is a professor at the School of Economics, Kwansei Gakuin University. His main areas of research interest are public finance, social security, and macroeconomics. He has published papers in scholarly journals including *Economics Letters*, *Economic Modelling*, *International Review of Economics* and *Journal of the Economics of Ageing*. Professor Yasuoka received a B.A. in economics from Nagoya City University and a Ph.D. in economics from Kobe University.

Chapter 3
Pay-As-You-Go Pension, Fertility, and Educational Investment

Masaya Yasuoka

1 Introduction

Japan's current pension system is operated under a modified funded scheme. The premiums collected from the working generation are directly used to fund the benefits for the retired generation. Additionally, reserve funds are drawn down to further support the benefits for the retired generation (Fig. 1).

Firstly, pension systems can be broadly divided into funded and pay-as-you-go schemes. The funded scheme involves setting aside a portion of one's income as insurance premiums during their working years. These premiums are then invested as reserve funds, and when the individual reaches old age, the principal and investment returns from these premiums are paid out as pension benefits. In this case, the premiums are invested, and the returns are determined by interest rates. Naturally, the return rates vary depending on how the assets are managed. The uncertainty of these return rates has been analyzed by scholars such as Borgmann (2005) and Yasuoka and Oshio (2008). If no investment is made and the funds are simply kept, the reserve funds will decrease in value by the rate of inflation. Active investment may involve putting money into high-risk stocks or foreign exchange, which could yield substantial returns or result in significant losses. However, the current issue of Japan's declining population does not directly pose a problem as long as the funded scheme is in place (Fig. 2).

The pay-as-you-go scheme involves using the insurance premiums paid by the current working generation to fund the pension benefits for the existing elderly generation. In this case, the return rate of the pension is equivalent to the population growth rate. The more numerous the working generation compared to the elderly generation, the larger the benefits received per elderly individual (Fig. 3).

M. Yasuoka (✉)
School of Economics, Kwansei Gakuin University, Nishinomiya, Japan
e-mail: yasuoka@kwansei.ac.jp

M. Jinno and M. Yasuoka (eds.), *Fertility, Education and Macroeconomics: The Case of Japan*, https://doi.org/10.1007/978-981-95-1024-5_3

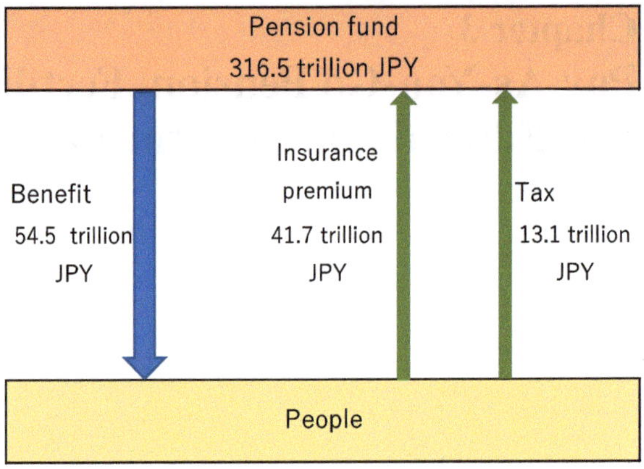

Fig. 1 The operation of the current pension system in Japan. *Source* Ministry of Health, Labour and Welfare (2025)

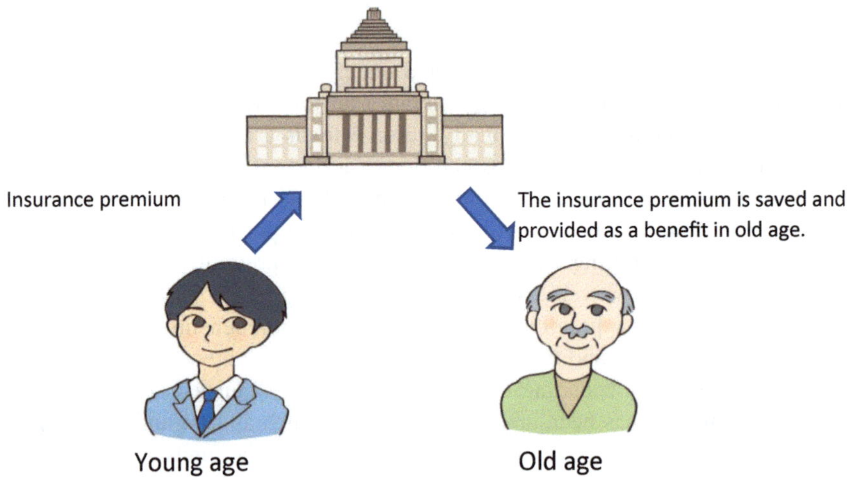

Fig. 2 Fully funded pension system

Thus, the modified funded scheme can be seen as a hybrid of the funded and pay-as-you-go schemes. When elements of the pay-as-you-go scheme are incorporated into Japan's pension system, the population level, particularly the birth rate that influences it, becomes a significant issue.

Originally, in the absence of a pension system, people had to rely on their children for living expenses and care in old age. However, the pension system has eliminated the need for children to provide such support, leading to a decrease in the number of children. This in turn results in a lower population growth rate, which paradoxically undermines the sustainability of the pension system, as explained by Zhang and Nishimura (1993), and Oshio and Yasuoka (2009).

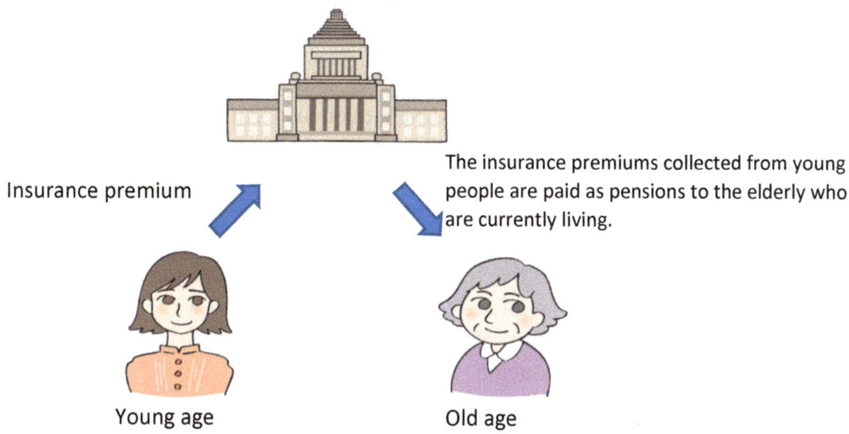

Fig. 3 Pay-As-You-Go pension system

Models that do not consider parental care by children and endogenize birth rates and pensions have been analyzed by van Groezen, Leers, and Meijdam (2003) and Oshio and Yasuoka (2009). Additionally, investment in children's education can increase the level of future human capital, which, similar to an increase in birth rates, has the effect of increasing pension benefits received in old age. This is explained by Yasuoka and Miyake (2014).

Furthermore, regarding the relationship between pension premiums and benefits, there are two approaches: the fixed premium scheme (defined contribution pension), where premiums are fixed, and benefits are determined to meet the government's budget constraint; and the fixed benefit scheme (defined benefit pension), where benefits are fixed, and premiums are determined to meet the government's budget constraint. This chapter presents a model based on endogenous birth rates and a defined contribution pension scheme, and then develops a model that considers investment in children's education in addition to endogenous birth rates, explaining a series of studies.

The remainder of this chapter is organized as follows. Section 2 explains an endogenous fertility model with pensions. Section 3 examines the case of defined benefit pensions and fertility. Section 4 considers education investment for children in the context of pensions. Section 5 explains defined contribution pensions and education investment for children. Section 6 considers the case of pensions as an incentive to have children. In the final section, we discuss the results and related literature.

2 Endogenous Fertility Model with Pension

In this section, we will explain the setup of an endogenous fertility model that considers the pension system. Although the endogenous fertility model that includes the pension system has been established in various works, we set the model based on Yasuoka (2006).

First, let us establish the simplest model for analyzing childcare support policies. In this model, there are three economic agents: households, firms, and the government. Individuals in households live through two periods: youth and old age. During their youth, they inelastically supply one unit of labor and earn a wage w_t.. However, from this wage, a tax for childcare support (with a tax rate τ) and a pension premium (with a premium rate ε) are deducted. The income remaining after these deductions is then allocated to youth consumption $c_{y,t}$, childcare expenditures, and savings s_t for consumption in old age $c_{o,t+1}$.

The cost of raising one child is denoted as z_t, and the benefit received per child under childcare support policies is q_t. When the number of children is n_t, the net childcare expenditure, taking into account the benefits, is $(z_t - q_t)n_t$. Here, t denotes the period, and individuals who are young in period t will be old in period $t+1$. The budget constraint during the youth period is thus represented as follows:

$$c_{y,t} + (z_t - q_t)n_t + s_t = (1 - \tau - \varepsilon)w_t. \tag{1}$$

Next, we consider the behavior during old age. In old age, individuals do not work, and their consumption is covered by the principal and interest on their savings, as well as the pension benefits P_{t+1}. The budget constraint during the old age period is represented as follows:

$$c_{o,t+1} = (1 + r_{t+1})s_t + P_{t+1}. \tag{2}$$

$c_{o,t+1}$ and r_{t+1} denote the consumption in old age period and the interest rate. By changing (2) and substituting $s_t = \frac{c_{o,t+1}}{1+r_{t+1}} - \frac{P_{t+1}}{1+r_{t+1}}$ into (1), we show the lifetime budget constraint as follows:

$$c_{y,t} + (z_t - q_t)n_t + \frac{c_{o,t+1}}{1 + r_{t+1}} = (1 - \tau - \varepsilon)w_t + \frac{P_{t+1}}{1 + r_{t+1}}. \tag{3}$$

Now, regarding the utility function, we assume it as follows:

$$u_t = \alpha \ln n_t + \beta \ln c_{y,t} + (1 - \alpha - \beta)\ln c_{o,t+1}, \quad 0 < \alpha < 1, \quad 0 < \beta < 1, \quad \alpha + \beta < 1. \tag{4}$$

Subject to the budget constraint (3), individuals in households choose the allocation of consumption and the number of children to maximize the utility function (4). The Lagrangian function can be set up as follows:

$$L = \alpha \ln n_t + \beta \ln c_{y,t} + (1-\alpha-\beta)\ln c_{o,t+1} + \lambda\left((1-\tau-\varepsilon)w_t + \frac{P_{t+1}}{1+r_{t+1}} - c_{y,t} - (z_t - q_t)n_t - \frac{c_{o,t+1}}{1+r}\right). \quad (5)$$

The necessary conditions for the optimal solution are as follows:

$$\frac{\partial L}{\partial n_t} = \frac{\alpha}{n_t} - \lambda(z_t - q_t) = 0 \rightarrow \frac{\alpha}{\lambda} = (z_t - q_t)n_t, \quad (6)$$

$$\frac{\partial L}{\partial c_{y,t}} = \frac{\beta}{c_{y,t}} - \lambda = 0 \rightarrow \frac{\beta}{\lambda} = c_{y,t}, \quad (7)$$

$$\frac{\partial L}{\partial c_{o,t+1}} = \frac{1-\alpha-\beta}{c_{o,t+1}} - \frac{\lambda}{1+r_{t+1}} = 0 \rightarrow \frac{1-\alpha-\beta}{\lambda} = \frac{c_{o,t+1}}{1+r_{t+1}}, \quad (8)$$

$$\frac{\partial L}{\partial \lambda} = (1-\tau-\varepsilon)w_t + \frac{P_{t+1}}{1+r_{t+1}} - c_{y,t} - (z_t - q_t)n_t - \frac{c_{o,t+1}}{1+r_{t+1}} = 0. \quad (9)$$

These are called the first-order conditions, which are the necessary conditions for the optimal solution. By substituting Eqs. (6)–(8) into the budget constraint (3), we obtain the following equation:

$$\frac{1}{\lambda} = (1-\tau-\varepsilon)w_t + \frac{P_{t+1}}{1+r_{t+1}}. \quad (10)$$

Therefore, by substituting Eq. (10) into Eqs. (7)–(9), the number of children and consumption are determined as follows:

$$n_t = \frac{\alpha\left((1-\tau-\varepsilon)w_t + \frac{P_{t+1}}{1+r_{t+1}}\right)}{z_t - q_t}, \quad (11)$$

$$c_{y,t} = \beta\left((1-\tau-\varepsilon)w_t + \frac{P_{t+1}}{1+r_{t+1}}\right), \quad (12)$$

$$c_{o,t+1} = (1+r_{t+1})(1-\alpha-\beta)\left((1-\tau-\varepsilon)w_t + \frac{P_{t+1}}{1+r_{t+1}}\right). \quad (13)$$

If the number of the younger generation is N_t and each individual in the younger generation has n_t children, the necessary cost for the childcare support policy is $q_t N_t n_t$. The total amount of labor income tax collected from the younger generation is $\tau N_t w_t$. Assuming the policy operates with a balanced budget, the following equation holds:

$$\tau N_t w_t = q_t N_t n_t \rightarrow \tau w_t = q_t n_t. \quad (14)$$

Here, we assume that the per capita childcare cost and the benefits of childcare support are proportional to the wages as follows:

$$z_t = \overline{z}w_t, 0 < \overline{z}, \tag{15}$$

$$q_t = \overline{q}w_t, 0 < \overline{q}. \tag{16}$$

By substituting Eqs. (15) and (16) into Eq. (11), we obtain the following equation:

$$n = \frac{\alpha\left((1-\tau-\varepsilon) + \frac{P_{t+1}}{w_t(1+r_{t+1})}\right)}{\overline{z}-\overline{q}}. \tag{17}$$

Next, let's consider the profit-maximizing behavior of firms. We assume the following production function:

$$Y_t = K_t^{\theta} L_t^{1-\theta}, \quad 0 < \theta < 1. \tag{18}$$

Given that Y_t is the output, K_t is the capital stock, and L_t is the labor input, and assuming that capital is completely depreciated in one period, firms maximize their profit π_t. The profit can be formulated as follows:

$$\pi_t = K_t^{\theta} L_t^{1-\theta} - (1+r_t)K_t - w_t L_t. \tag{19}$$

Therefore, considering profit maximization, the wage rate and the interest rate can be derived from the marginal products of labor and capital, respectively. These can be expressed as follows:

$$w_t = (1-\theta)k_t^{\theta}, k_t = \frac{K_t}{L_t}, \tag{20}$$

$$1 + r_t = \theta k_t^{\theta-1}. \tag{21}$$

The equilibrium condition in the capital market can be expressed as follows:

$$K_{t+1} = N_t s_t \rightarrow n_t k_{t+1} = s_t \rightarrow n_t k_{t+1} = (1-\tau)w_t - (z-q)n_t - c_{y,t}. \tag{22}$$

$n_t = \frac{N_{t+1}}{N_t}$ is given. Given that N_t and N_{t+1} represent the population size of the younger generation in periods t and $t+1$ respectively, substituting Eqs. (11) and (12) into (22), we can derive the dynamic equation for capital stock as follows:

$$n_t k_{t+1} = (1-\alpha-\beta)(1-\tau-\varepsilon)w_t - \frac{(\alpha+\beta)P_{t+1}}{1+r_{t+1}}. \tag{23}$$

Now, we consider a defined contribution pension system, where the premium rate is fixed and the benefits are determined according to the government's budget constraint. Under this system, the relationship between the premium rate and the benefits can be expressed as follows:

$$N_t p_{t+1} = \varepsilon N_{t+1} w_{t+1} \rightarrow P_{t+1} = \varepsilon n_t w_{t+1}. \tag{24}$$

Note that N_t represents the population size of the younger generation in period t, but in period $t+1$, it represents the population size of the elderly generation. By substituting Eqs. (20), (21), and (24) into (23), we obtain the following equation:

$$\frac{n_t k_{t+1}}{w_t} = \frac{(1-\alpha-\beta)(1-\tau-\varepsilon)}{1+\frac{\varepsilon(\alpha+\beta)(1-\theta)}{\theta}}. \tag{25}$$

The part $\frac{P_{t+1}}{w_t(1+r_{t+1})}$ of (17) changes to $\frac{\varepsilon(1-\theta)n_t k_{t+1}}{\theta w_t}$. Then, from Eqs. (17) and (25), the number of children can ultimately be expressed as follows:

$$n = \frac{\alpha(1-\tau-\varepsilon)\left(1+\frac{\varepsilon(1-\theta)(1-\alpha-\beta)}{\theta+\varepsilon(\alpha+\beta)(1-\theta)}\right)}{\overline{z}-\overline{q}} \rightarrow n = \frac{\alpha\left((1-\varepsilon)+\frac{\varepsilon(1-\alpha-\beta)(1-\tau-\varepsilon)}{\theta+\varepsilon(\alpha+\beta)(1-\theta)}\right)}{\overline{z}-(1-\alpha)\overline{q}}. \tag{26}$$

From Eqs. (25) and (26), it can be concluded that the dynamic equation for capital is ultimately expressed as follows:

$$k_{t+1} = \frac{(1-\alpha-\beta)(1-\theta)(1-\tau-\varepsilon)}{n\left(1+\frac{\varepsilon(\alpha+\beta)(1-\theta)}{\theta}\right)} k_t^{\theta}. \tag{27}$$

Therefore, the capital stock converges to a steady-state capital stock k over time, but the number of children remains constant over time, regardless of the level of capital stock. It is found that the childcare support benefit $\overline{q}$ increases the number of children n. As for the capital stock, the steady-state capital stock can be expressed by substituting $k_{t+1} = k_t = k$ into Eq. (27) as follows:

$$k = \left(\frac{(1-\alpha-\beta)(1-\theta)(1-\tau-\varepsilon)}{n\left(1+\frac{\varepsilon(\alpha+\beta)(1-\theta)}{\theta}\right)}\right)^{\frac{1}{1-\theta}}. \tag{28}$$

It is found that the childcare support benefit $\overline{q}$ increases the capital stock k. The effect of childcare support benefits is essentially the same whether or not pensions are included when considering this defined contribution pension system. So, what effect would an increase in the pension premium rate ε have?

First, according to Eq. (28), an increase in the pension premium rate ε would decrease the capital stock. This is because higher pension benefits reduce the need for individual savings, which in turn reduces investment and thus decreases the capital stock. Consequently, as the future pension premium income decreases due to the reduction in capital stock, the effect of a balanced budget operation with a fixed premium rate results in reduced pension benefits.

Therefore, while an increase in the pension premium rate could directly increase disposable income, its impact on the number of children is uncertain due to the two opposing effects on lifetime income. The reduction in pension benefits due to the decreased capital stock, as reflected in the number of children in Eq. (27), makes the overall impact on the number of children unclear.

3 Defined Benefit Pension and Fertility

In this section, we will determine the number of children in the case where the pension benefit scheme is a defined benefit system. For simplicity, we will develop the model by considering a small open economy based on the work of Oshio and Yasuoka (2009). Although their work analyzes a closed economy, the essential results remain unchanged.

Regarding the pension benefit level, it is fixed at a proportion δ of the wage. Meanwhile, the pension premium rate is ε. Therefore, in the case of a defined benefit pension, the following relationship exists between the premiums and benefits:

$$N_t \varepsilon w = N_{t-1} P_t \rightarrow N_t \varepsilon w = N_{t-1} \delta w \rightarrow \varepsilon = \frac{\delta}{n_{t-1}}. \tag{29}$$

$n_{t-1} = \frac{N_t}{N_{t-1}}$ is given. By substituting Eq. (29) into Eq. (17), we can obtain the number of children as follows:

$$n_t = \frac{\alpha\left(\left(1 - \frac{\delta}{n_{t-1}}\right) + \frac{\delta}{1+r}\right)}{\overline{z} - (1-\alpha)\overline{q}}. \tag{30}$$

As can be seen from Eq. (30), a dynamic process occurs for the number of children in the case of a defined benefit pension. This is because pension premiums depend on the population size of the younger generation. If the population size of the younger generation is large, that is, if n_{t-1} is large, the per capita premium burden for the younger generation is small, so the negative impact on disposable income is small, and the number of children n_t increases.

If Eq. (30) has a steady-state number of children n where $n_{t-1} = n_t = n$, the following dynamics can be drawn.

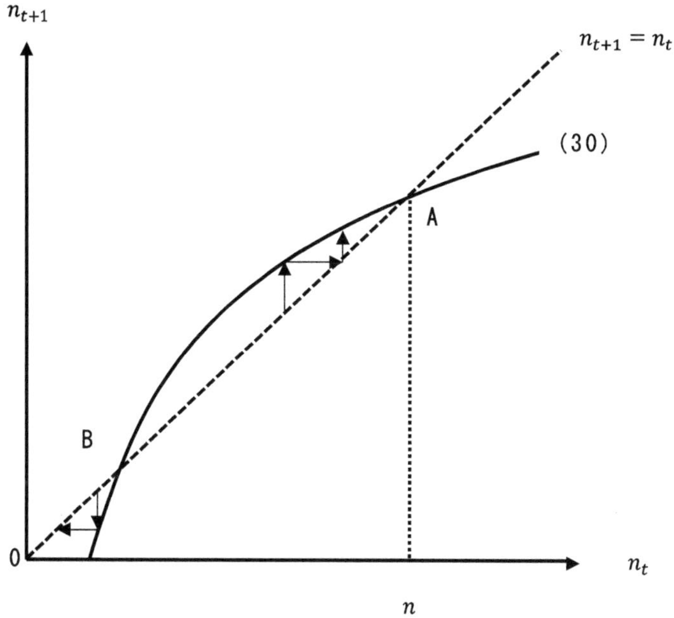

Fig. 4 Dynamics of n_t

As shown in Fig. 4, generally, when a steady state exists, it is possible to obtain two steady state numbers of children.[1] However, among the two steady state equilibria, A and B, equilibrium A is a stable steady-state, while equilibrium B is an unstable steady state. Therefore, if the number of children is less than that at equilibrium B, the number of children will continue to decrease over time. On the other hand, if the number of children is greater than that at equilibrium B, it will converge to the number of children at equilibrium A over time. This result is intuitive. When the number of children is small, the per capita pension premium burden on the younger generation is high, which means there are insufficient expenditures available for childcare, resulting in a smaller number of children. Consequently, in the next period, the pension premium increases further, reducing the household's disposable income even more, and making it even more challenging to allocate sufficient expenditures for childcare (Fig. 5).

---

[1] We can obtain the fertility at the steady state (30) and $n = \frac{\alpha\left(1+\frac{\delta}{1+r}\right) \pm \sqrt{\alpha^2\left(1+\frac{\delta}{1+r}\right)^2 - 4\alpha\delta(\overline{z}-(1-\alpha)\overline{q})}}{2(\overline{z}-(1-\alpha)\overline{q})}$, which is considered as $n_t = n_{t-1} = n$, and we solve quadratic function $(\overline{z} - (1-\alpha)\overline{q})n^2 - \alpha\left(1 + \frac{\delta}{1+r}\right)n + \alpha\delta = 0$. In this case, the stable steady-state number of children is the one with the positive sign before the square root. Additionally, for the condition to have a steady-state, the quadratic equation must have real solutions. Therefore, the condition is $\alpha^2\left(1 + \frac{\delta}{1+r}\right)^2 - 4\alpha\delta(\overline{z} - (1-\alpha)\overline{q}) > 0$.

① When the population size of the younger generation is small, the burden of insurance premiums increases.

↓

② Due to the heavy burden of insurance premiums, disposable income decreases.

↓

③ Due to the limited disposable income, sufficient spending on child-rearing is not possible.

↓

④ The number of children decreases.

↓

⑤ The population size of the younger generation in the next period decreases.

Fig. 5 The Negative Spiral of Declining Birth Rates and Increasing Insurance Premiums

In reality, such a negative spiral is conceivable. It is challenging to reduce social security benefits in Japan, and often the response is to increase the burden instead. This places a significant burden on the working generation, reducing their disposable income. Consequently, they are forced to cut back on expenditures for childcare, leading to a decrease in the number of children and further accelerating the decline in birth rates.

If a steady state does not exist, it can be considered that $\overline{z}$ is quite high and it is not possible to sufficiently increase the number of children. In this case, the dynamics are shown in Fig. 6. In this scenario, the number of children will continue to decrease over time. One method to stop this trend is to eliminate the defined benefit pension system, thereby removing the premium burden on the younger generation. Another method is to increase the level of childcare support benefit $\overline{q}$. By doing so, it is possible to increase the number of children n_t for any given n_{t-1} (see Fig. 6), ensuring the existence of a steady-state number of children and halting the continuous decline in the birth rate (Fig. 7).

4 Education Investment in Endogenous Fertility with Pension

In Yasuoka and Miyake (2014), the so-called quantity and quality model of children, which incorporates educational investment into an endogenous birth rate model, was used to examine pay-as-you-go pensions. When educational investment affects human capital, it increases labor productivity through the growth of human capital,

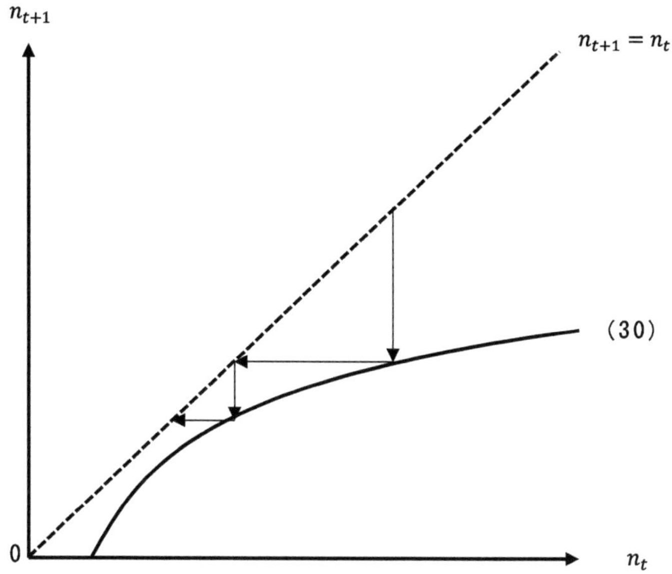

Fig. 6 Dynamics of n_t (no steady state)

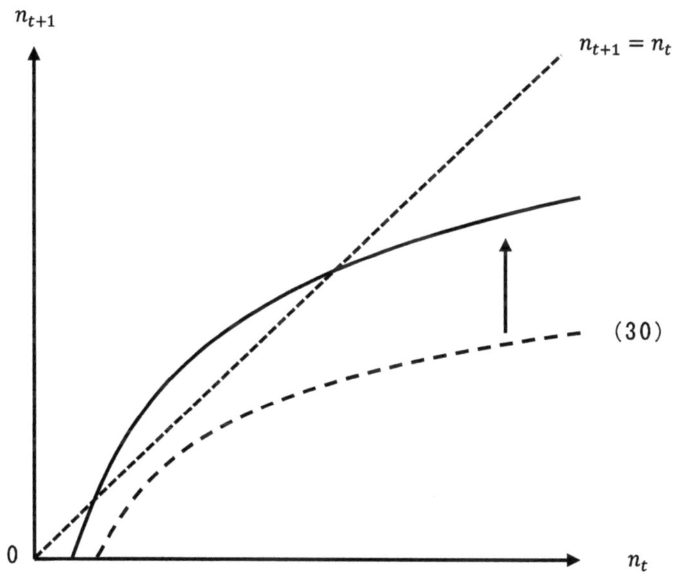

Fig. 7 Dynamics of n_t and childcare support

thereby increasing labor income. This results in income growth, and for pay-as-you-go pensions, the rate of return includes not only the birth rate but also the income growth rate.

Now, let's set up the model based on Yasuoka (2008) and Yasuoka and Miyake (2014), considering a small open economy.

First, individuals in households live for two periods: youth and old age. During their youth, they supply one unit of labor inelastically and earn labor income. At this time, labor income is given by wh_t, where w is the wage rate per unit of human capital, and h_t is the level of human capital. The earned labor income is then subject to deductions for taxes for childcare support and premiums for pension benefits, with tax rate τ and premium rate γ, respectively.

The cost of raising an additional child, called the childcare cost, is z_t, and the benefit from childcare support is q_t. The number of children is n_t. The educational investment per child is e_t. During the youth period, when individuals allocate resources for child-rearing, consumption $c_{y,t}$, and savings s_t for old-age consumption $c_{o,t+1}$, the budget constraint for the youth period is as follows:

$$(z_t - q_t)n_t + e_t n_t + c_{y,t} + s_t = (1 - \tau - \gamma)wh_t. \tag{31}$$

Next, in the old age period, individuals use the principal and interest from their savings, as well as pension benefits, for consumption. Let the interest rate on savings be r, and the pension benefit amount be P_{t+1}. The budget constraint for the old age period is as follows:

$$(1 + r)s_t + P_{t+1} = c_{o,t+1}. \tag{32}$$

From Eqs. (31) and (32), the lifetime budget constraint can be expressed as follows:

$$(z_t - q_t)n_t + e_t n_t + c_{y,t} + \frac{c_{o,t+1}}{1+r} = (1 - \tau - \gamma)wh_t + \frac{P_{t+1}}{1+r}. \tag{33}$$

Based on de la Croix and Doepke (2003), we assume the following utility function:

$$u_t = \alpha \ln n_t h_{t+1} + \beta \ln c_{y,t} + (1 - \alpha - \beta)\ln c_{o,t+1}. \tag{34}$$

Here, h_{t+1} represents the human capital of the children. The utility is influenced not only by the number of children but also by the level of human capital resulting from educational investment in the children. The children's human capital h_{t+1} is considered to be determined by the educational investment e_t and the parent's human capital h_t. We assume the following human capital function:

$$h_{t+1} = e_t^{\varepsilon} h_t^{1-\varepsilon}, \quad 0 < \varepsilon < 1. \tag{35}$$

To maximize the utility function (34) subject to the constraints (33) and (35), we can set up the Lagrangian function as follows[2]:

$$L = \alpha \ln n_t + \alpha\varepsilon \ln e_t + \alpha(1-\varepsilon)\ln h_t + \beta \ln c_{y,t} + (1-\alpha-\beta)\ln c_{o,t+1}$$
$$+\lambda\left((1-\tau-\varepsilon)wh_t + \frac{P_{t+1}}{1+r} - c_{y,t} - (z_t - q_t)n_t - \frac{c_{o,t+1}}{1+r} - e_t n_t\right). \quad (36)$$

The necessary conditions for the optimal solution are as follows:

$$\frac{\partial L}{\partial n_t} = \frac{\alpha}{n_t} - \lambda(z_t - q_t + e_t) = 0 \rightarrow \frac{\alpha}{\lambda} = (z_t - q_t)n_t + e_t n_t, \quad (37)$$

$$\frac{\partial L}{\partial e_t} = \frac{\alpha\varepsilon}{e_t} - \lambda n_t = 0 \rightarrow \frac{\alpha\varepsilon}{\lambda} = e_t n_t, \quad (38)$$

$$\frac{\partial L}{\partial c_{y,t}} = \frac{\beta}{c_{y,t}} - \lambda = 0 \rightarrow \frac{\beta}{\lambda} = c_{y,t}, \quad (39)$$

$$\frac{\partial L}{\partial c_{o,t+1}} = \frac{1-\alpha-\beta}{c_{o,t+1}} - \frac{\lambda}{1+r_{t+1}} = 0 \rightarrow \frac{1-\alpha-\beta}{\lambda} = \frac{c_{o,t+1}}{1+r}. \quad (40)$$

By substituting Eqs. (37), (39), and (40) into (33), we obtain the following equation:

$$\frac{1}{\lambda} = (1-\tau-\varepsilon)wh_t + \frac{P_{t+1}}{1+r}. \quad (41)$$

From Eqs. (37) and (38), the educational investment in children can be expressed as follows:

$$e_t = \frac{\varepsilon(z_t - q_t)}{1-\varepsilon}. \quad (42)$$

Here, the childcare cost z_t and the childcare support benefit q_t can be expressed in a form proportional to wages as follows:

$$z_t = \bar{z}wh_t, 0 < \bar{z}, \quad (43)$$

$$q_t = \bar{q}wh_t, 0 < \bar{q}. \quad (44)$$

Additionally, if pension benefits are provided as defined contributions, the relationship between the premium rate and pension benefits is as follows:

---

[2] $\alpha \ln h_{t+1} = \alpha \ln e_t^{\varepsilon} h_t^{1-\varepsilon} = \alpha \ln e_t^{\varepsilon} + \alpha \ln h_t^{1-\varepsilon} = \alpha\varepsilon \ln e_t + \alpha(1-\varepsilon)\ln h_t$ can be shown as a property of logarithms.

$$N_{t+1}\gamma wh_{t+1} = N_t P_{t+1} \to P_{t+1} = n_t \gamma wh_{t+1}. \tag{45}$$

By substituting Eqs. (38), (41), (43), (44), and (45) into (37), the number of children can be given as follows:

$$n = \frac{\alpha(1-\varepsilon)\left((1-\tau-\gamma) + \frac{\gamma n(1+g)}{1+r}\right)}{\overline{z} - \overline{q}}. \tag{46}$$

$1+g = \frac{h_{t+1}}{h_t}$ is given, as is the growth rate of human capital stock. Additionally, the budget constraint equation for childcare support benefits is:

$$\tau N_t wh_t = q_t N_t n_t \to \tau = \overline{q}n. \tag{47}$$

Therefore, substituting this into Eq. (46), we obtain the following equation:

$$n = \frac{\alpha(1-\varepsilon)\left((1-\gamma) + \frac{\gamma n(1+g)}{1+r}\right)}{\overline{z} - (1-\alpha(1-\varepsilon))\overline{q}}. \tag{48}$$

where

$$1+g = \frac{h_{t+1}}{h_t} = \left(\frac{e_t}{h_t}\right)^{\varepsilon} = \left(\frac{\varepsilon w(\overline{z}-\overline{q})}{1-\varepsilon}\right)^{\varepsilon}. \tag{49}$$

Therefore, when considering pension benefits, the growth rate of income decreases due to childcare support benefits, which in turn reduces the rate of return on pensions. This results in a decrease in disposable income over an individual's lifetime, leading to a reduction in the number of children. By totally differentiating Eqs. (47) and (48) with $\overline{q} = 0$, we can obtain the following equation:

$$\frac{dn}{d\overline{q}} = \frac{n\left(1 - \alpha - \frac{\alpha\gamma\varepsilon(1-\varepsilon)(1+g)}{(1+r)\overline{z}}\right)}{\overline{z} - \frac{\alpha\gamma(1-\varepsilon)(1+g)}{1+r}}. \tag{50}$$

The first term in the numerator indicates the direct increase in the number of children due to childcare support benefits. However, in the presence of a defined contribution pension system, the existence of childcare support benefits leads to a substitution effect, where educational investment in children decreases instead of increasing the number of children. This reduces the growth rate of income, which in turn decreases pension benefits, leading to a reduction in the household's disposable income. As a result, expenditures on childcare decrease.

Therefore, in the presence of a defined contribution pension system, the effectiveness of childcare support policies is weakened (Fig. 8).

The effect of childcare support benefits on the number of children can also be illustrated with the following dynamics (Fig. 9).

Increase in childcare support benefits

↓ ↓

① Direct effect

Since the net cost of raising children decreases, the number of children increases.

↓

② Indirect effect

By reducing the rate of income growth, pension benefits decrease, resulting in a reduction of lifetime income, which in turn decreases the number of children.

↓

The magnitude of the final effect is determined.

Fig. 8 Summary of the effects of childcare support benefits in defined contribution pension

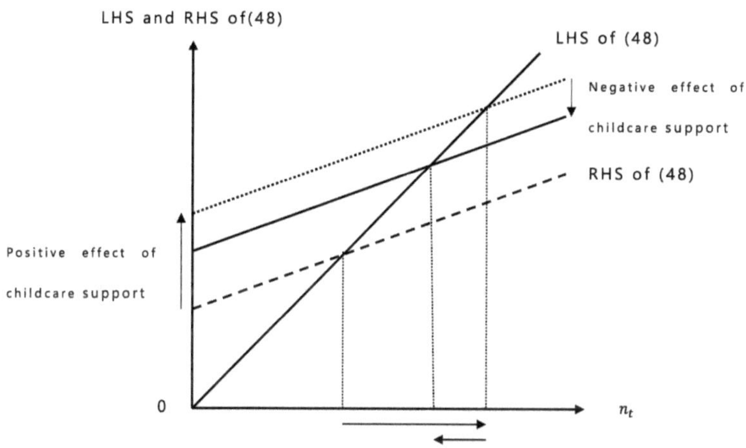

Fig. 9 Childcare support and the number of children

The positive effect of increasing childcare support benefits is the direct increase in the number of children. However, the negative effect of childcare support benefits, which is the reduction in the growth rate of income leading to a decrease in the number of children, weakens the overall effect of increasing childcare support benefits.

5 Defined Contribution Pension and Education Investment for Children

In this section, let's consider the determination of the number of children and educational investment for individuals in households when pension benefits are provided as defined benefit pensions. First, regarding the relationship between premiums and pension benefits in a defined benefit pension system, we assume that individuals who were part of the younger generation in period t receive pension benefits in period $t+1$ equal to a proportion δ of their income wh_{t+1}. In this case, $P_{t+1} = \delta wh_{t+1}$. Therefore, the following equation holds:

$$N_{t+1}\gamma wh_{t+1} = N_t P_{t+1} \rightarrow \gamma = \frac{\delta}{n_{t-1}}. \tag{51}$$

At this time, Eq. (41) is modified as follows:

$$\frac{1}{\lambda} = \left(1 - \tau - \frac{\delta}{n_{t-1}}\right) wh_t + \frac{\delta wh_{t+1}}{1+r}. \tag{52}$$

By following a similar procedure as for deriving Eq. (46) or (48), the number of children can be derived as follows:

$$n_t = \frac{\alpha(1-\varepsilon)\left(\left(1 - \frac{\delta}{n_{t-1}}\right) + \frac{\delta(1+g)}{1+r}\right)}{\overline{z} - (1 - \alpha(1-\varepsilon))\overline{q}}. \tag{53}$$

Similar to Sect. 3, in the case of defined benefit pensions, dynamic changes in the fertility occur. The reason is similar to that in Sect. 3, where the relative population size of the younger generation to the elderly generation affects the pension premiums paid by the younger generation, which in turn changes disposable income and subsequently the number of children.

The effect of increasing childcare support benefits is similar to that in the case of defined contribution pensions. Since the denominator in Eq. (53) includes the childcare support benefit $\overline{q}$, there is an effect of increasing the number of children n_t for any given n_{t-1}. However, the presence of the income growth rate $1+g$ in the numerator weakens the effect of childcare support benefits on increasing the number of children. This is similar to the case of defined contribution pensions.

In the case of defined benefit pensions, special attention must be given to the existence of a steady state.

Figure 10 illustrates the effect of increasing the birth rate in the context of defined benefit pensions. The dashed curve represents the number of children before implementing childcare support benefits, as indicated by Eq. (53). With the increase in childcare support benefits, the number of children n_t rises for a given n_{t-1}, and as shown by the dotted curve, a steady state is achieved—this was the analysis in the defined benefit pension model without considering educational investment.

However, when educational investment is included, and the growth rate of income decreases due to childcare support benefits, an additional effect of reducing the number of children occurs. Despite the direct effect of increasing the number of children through childcare support benefits, which establishes a steady state and halts the ongoing decrease in the number of children, the indirect effect of reducing the number of children due to decreased income growth results in the loss of the

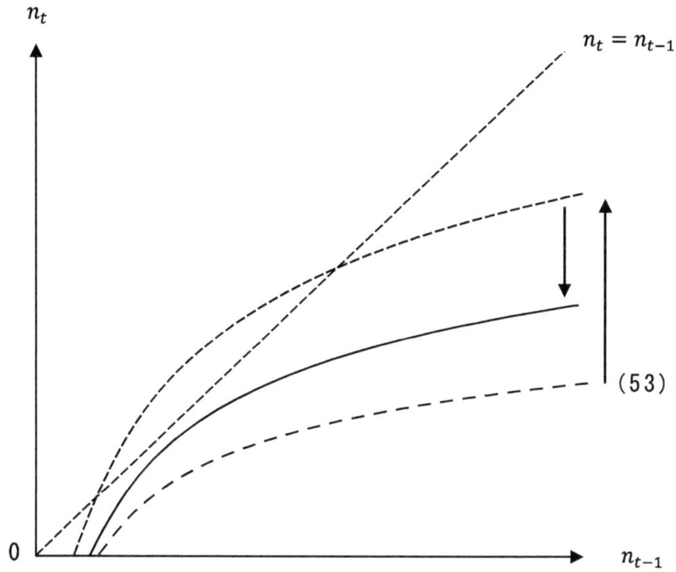

Fig. 10 Childcare support and defined benefit pension

steady state. Consequently, the continued path of decreasing number of children cannot be halted. Therefore, it is necessary to consider this when determining the level of childcare support benefits.

6 Pension of an Incentive to Have Children

It is possible to increase the birth rate or the level of educational investment through child allowances or educational subsidy policies. However, it does not make a difference whether these benefits are provided in kind or in cash, as long as the benefits are proportional to the number of children or the amount of educational investment in children. Therefore, providing the benefits as pensions in old age instead of as childcare support during youth would essentially have the same effect.

In other words, if the birth rate and human capital levels increase, individuals can receive higher pension benefits under a defined contribution pension system with fixed premiums. If the birth rate and human capital levels chosen by individuals increase, it will result in higher pension benefits. In other words, if other households raise more children and make active educational investments, the pension benefits received by individuals will increase. This suggests that pensions have externalities, particularly positive externalities. When positive externalities are present, the government can enhance social welfare by providing subsidies. These subsidies can be provided not only as direct childcare support to the younger generation but also as pension benefits to the elderly.

Indeed, previous studies have analyzed how the birth rate and educational investment in children are determined by systems where having more children or investing in education increases the pension benefits one receives. Notable papers include those of Fenge and Meier (2005), Meier and Wrede (2010), and Yasuoka (2018). Here, we present a simplified version of the model based on Yasuoka (2018) to analyze pension systems that incentivize the number of children and educational investment.

As mentioned above, whether benefits are received as childcare support during youth or as pension benefits during old age does not fundamentally affect lifetime income, as long as the impact on lifetime income remains unchanged. However, this holds true only in the absence of borrowing constraints. The model in this chapter assumes no borrowing constraints, meaning that individuals can borrow during their youth when expenses exceed income and repay during old age.

Therefore, the substitution of childcare support benefits with pension benefits during old age is feasible only if there are no borrowing constraints. If individuals face borrowing constraints during their youth and can only make limited expenditures for childcare, they will not be able to increase the number of children or educational investment. Consequently, even if pension benefits with the effect of childcare support are provided during old age, there may be little impact.

In summary, we have discussed the timing of benefits for children across generations. In this section, we will analyze a pension system with the effect of childcare support benefits using a simplified version of the work of Yasuoka (2018), assuming no borrowing constraints.

Firstly, regarding the structure of the model, individuals in households live for two periods: youth and old age. Each period features an overlapping generations model where the younger and older generations coexist. The budget constraint during youth is considered as follows:

$$z_t n_t + e_t n_t + c_{y,t} + s_t = (1 - \mu) w h_t. \tag{54}$$

Let w be the wage rate per unit of human capital, h_t be the level of human capital, z_t be the childcare cost per child, n_t be the number of children, e_t be the educational investment per child, $c_{y,t}$ be the consumption during youth, s_t be the savings, and μ be the pension premium rate.

Next, for the old age period, individuals use the principal and interest from their savings, as well as the pension benefits, for consumption. Let the interest rate on savings be r, the consumption during old age be $c_{o,t+1}$, and the pension benefit amount be $\mu n_t w h_{t+1}$. The budget constraint for the old age period is as follows:

$$(1 + r) s_t + \mu n_t w h_{t+1} = c_{o,t+1}. \tag{55}$$

Additionally, h_{t+1} represents the level of human capital of the children, which increases due to educational investment. Here, the term $\mu n_t w h_{t+1}$ reflects the pension benefits influenced by the number of children and the educational investment chosen. If the number of children or educational investment increases, the pension benefit $n_t w h_{t+1}$ will also increase, resulting in higher income.

From Eqs. (54) and (55), the lifetime budget constraint can be expressed as follows:

$$z_t n_t + e_t n_t + c_{y,t} + \frac{c_{o,t+1}}{1+r} = (1-\mu)wh_t + \frac{\mu n_t wh_{t+1}}{1+r}. \tag{56}$$

Given the utility function as in (34) and the human capital accumulation equation as in (35), the Lagrangian function to derive the optimal allocation can be set up as follows:

$$L = \alpha \ln n_t + \alpha\varepsilon \ln e_t + \alpha(1-\varepsilon)\ln h_t + \beta \ln c_{y,t} + (1-\alpha-\beta)\ln c_{o,t+1}$$
$$+ \lambda\left((1-\mu)wh_t + \frac{\mu n_t wh_{t+1}}{1+r} - c_{y,t} - z_t n_t - \frac{c_{o,t+1}}{1+r} - e_t n_t\right). \tag{57}$$

The necessary conditions for the optimal solution are as follows:

$$\frac{\partial L}{\partial n_t} = \frac{\alpha}{n_t} - \lambda\left(z_t + e_t - \frac{\mu wh_{t+1}}{1+r}\right) = 0 \to \frac{\alpha}{\lambda} = z_t n_t + e_t n_t - \frac{\mu n_t wh_{t+1}}{1+r}, \tag{58}$$

$$\frac{\partial L}{\partial e_t} = \frac{\alpha\varepsilon}{e_t} - \lambda\left(n_t - \frac{\mu\varepsilon n_t wh_{t+1}}{1+r}\frac{1}{e_t}\right) = 0 \to \frac{\alpha\varepsilon}{\lambda} = e_t n_t - \frac{\mu\varepsilon n_t wh_{t+1}}{1+r}, \tag{59}$$

$$\frac{\partial L}{\partial c_{y,t}} = \frac{\beta}{c_{y,t}} - \lambda = 0 \to \frac{\beta}{\lambda} = c_{y,t}, \tag{60}$$

$$\frac{\partial L}{\partial c_{o,t+1}} = \frac{1-\alpha-\beta}{c_{o,t+1}} - \frac{\lambda}{1+r_{t+1}} = 0 \to \frac{1-\alpha-\beta}{\lambda} = \frac{c_{o,t+1}}{1+r}. \tag{61}$$

By substituting Eqs. (58), (60), and (61) into (56), we obtain the following equation:

$$\frac{1}{\lambda} = (1-\mu)wh_t. \tag{62}$$

Here, we define the childcare cost z_t in the same wage-proportional form as Eq. (43). Given this, the educational investment in children from Eqs. (58) and (59) can be expressed as follows:

$$e = \frac{\varepsilon \bar{z} wh_t}{1-\varepsilon}. \tag{63}$$

From Eqs. (58), (62), and (63), the number of children can be expressed as follows:

$$n = \frac{\alpha(1-\mu)}{\frac{\bar{z}}{1-\varepsilon} - \frac{\mu(1+g)}{1+r}}. \tag{64}$$

where

$$1 + g = \left(\frac{\varepsilon \bar{z} h_t}{1 - \varepsilon} \right)^{\varepsilon}. \tag{65}$$

Therefore, it can be understood that if pension benefits include incentives to increase the number of children and educational investment, the number of children will increase.

However, on the other hand, educational investment is not affected. This can be attributed to the effect being absorbed by the increase in the number of children. If the number of children increases, the household's total educational investment in all children also increases. As a result, households are unlikely to choose to increase additional educational investment per child.

7 Conclusions

The model of endogenizing fertility rates, as discussed in previous chapters, is one where the number of children is directly included in utility, and this is referred to as the consumption goods model. On the other hand, there is also a model where children are treated as investment goods. In other words, the number of children is not directly included in the utility function; rather, the cost of raising children is considered along with the return (assistance from children to parents), which then determines the number of children. A specific example of such a model is Chakraborty and Das (2005), which takes into account not only fertility rates but also child labor and mortality rates. In this model, the more children one has, the more support one will receive from them in the future, providing an incentive to have more children. In other words, what this model suggests is that if there are systems like public pensions that can replace the support from children in old age, the income during old age can be substituted by these systems, which could reduce the demand for children as investment goods.

There is also a model where the inheritance from parents to children and the support from children to parents are determined based on strategic bequest motives. For example, Yakita (2024) considers a model of endogenous fertility rates where parents decide the size of the inheritance to their children based on the support they received from their children in old age. Futagami, Kamada, and Sato (2006) show that the fertility rate under strategic bequest motives is lower than that under altruistic bequest motives.

Although this book does not cover them, there are various motives for bequests. For example, there is the altruistic bequest motive, where the size of the bequest is determined in such a way that the utility function of the parent includes the utility function of the child, as analyzed by Barro and Becker (1989). Additionally, there is the bequest consumption model, where the size of the bequest itself is included in the parent's utility function.

Additionally, this chapter does not address income uncertainty. In reality, it is important to consider how the uncertainty of future income affects fertility rates.

Yasuoka (2021) has shown that the fertility rate is lower under income uncertainty compared to when there is no uncertainty. While this chapter does not present numerical calculations based on realistic parameters, the research itself has been conducted. For example, Ito et al. (2024a) demonstrate that appropriate social security benefits can increase the fertility rate even under future income uncertainty. In Ito et al. (2024b), although there is no income uncertainty, they use a human capital model that considers the number of children and investment in children's education to numerically clarify the extent to which policies can promote the number of children and the accumulation of human capital.

References

Barro, R. J., and Becker G. S. (1989). Fertility choice in a model of economic growth. *Econometrica, 57*(2), 481–501.

Borgmann, C. (2005). *Social security, demographics, and risk*. Springer-Verlag Berlin Heidelberg.

Chakraborty, S., and Das, M. (2005). Mortality, fertility, and child labor. *Economics Letters, 86*, 273–78.

de la Croix, D., and Doepke, M. (2003). Inequality and growth: Why differential fertility matters. *American Economic Review, 93*(4), 1091–1113.

Fenge, R., and Meier, V. (2005). Pensions and fertility incentives. *Canadian Journal of Economics, 38*(1), 28–48.

Futagami, R., Kamada, K., and Sato, T. (2006). Bequest motives and fertility decisions. *Economics Letters, 92*, 348–52.

Ito, T., Sako, K., Shiozu, Y., Jinno, M., and Yasuoka, M. (2024a). *Analysis of child care policies with an uncertainty model*. Discussion Paper Series 269, School of Economics, Kwansei Gakuin University.

Ito, T., Sako, K., Shiozu, Y., Jinno, M., and Yasuoka, M. (2024b). *Policy analysis in endogenous fertility model with human capital accumulation*. Discussion Paper Series 268, School of Economics, Kwansei Gakuin University.

Meier, V., and Wrede, M. (2010). Pensions, fertility, and education. *Journal of Pension Economics and Finance, 9*(1), 75–93.

Oshio, T., and Yasuoka, M. (2009). Maximum size of social security in a model of endogenous fertility. *Economics Bulletin, 29*(2), 656–66.

van Groezen, B., Leers, T., and Meijdam, L. (2003). Social security and endogenous fertility: Pensions and child allowances as Siamese twins. *Journal of Public Economics, 87*(2), 233–51.

Yakita, A. (2024). Old-age support policy and fertility with strategic bequest motives. *Journal of Population Economics, 37*(2), 1–23.

Yasuoka, M. (2006). Shusshouritsu to kazeiseisaku no kankei [The relationship between fertility rate and tax policy]. *Kikan Shakaihoshou Kenkyu* [*Quarterly of Social Security Research*], *42*(1), 80–90.

Yasuoka, M. (2008). Ikijishienseisaku no yukosei ni kansuru kosatsu [Analysis of effectiveness of childcare support policies]. *Studies in Applied Economics, 1*, 41–60.

Yasuoka, M. (2018). Fertility and education investment incentive with a pay-as-you-go pension. *Eurasian Economic Review, 8*(1), 37–50.

Yasuoka, M. (2021). Endogenous fertility and social security. *Keizai Kenkyu* [*Economic Analysis*], *202*, 201–19

Yasuoka, M., and Miyake, A. (2014). Fertility rate and child care policies in a pension system. *Economic Analysis and Policy, 44*(1), 122–27.

Yasuoka, M., and Oshio, T. (2008). The optimal and acceptable sizes of social security under uncertainty. *Japanese Journal of Social Security Policy*, *7*(1), 25–30.

Zhang, J., and Nishimura, K. (1993). The old-age hypothesis security revisited. *Journal of Development Economics*, *41*, 191–202.

Data

Ministry of Health, Labour and Welfare. (2025). Nenkinseido no pointo [Key points of the pension system 2025]. https://www.mhlw.go.jp/content/12500000/001475554.pdf

Masaya Yasuoka is a professor at the School of Economics, Kwansei Gakuin University. His main areas of research interest are public finance, social security, and macroeconomics. He has published papers in scholarly journals including *Economics Letters, Economic Modelling, International Review of Economics* and *Journal of the Economics of Ageing*. Professor Yasuoka received a B.A. in economics from Nagoya City University and a Ph.D. in economics from Kobe University.

Chapter 4
Fertility, Income Growth, and Inflation

Masaya Yasuoka

1 Introduction

In this chapter, we develop an endogenous fertility model that incorporates human capital accumulation through education investment for children. Additionally, we consider the impact of monetary policy within this model. Much of the related literature examines how childcare policies affect fertility and education investment for children.

Van Groezen et al. (2003) and Yasuoka and Goto (2011) examine the effect of child allowances on fertility in small open economy models. Conversely, in closed economy models that consider physical capital accumulation, such as those presented by van Groezen and Meijdam (2008), Fanti and Gori (2009), and Yasuoka and Goto (2015), child allowances reduce fertility due to a decrease in physical capital accumulation. Miyazaki (2013) investigates the effect of pensions on fertility.

We consider the effect of subsidies for education investment. Glomm and Ravikumar (1992) propose a model where public education investment fully covers education costs through government expenditure, thereby reducing the inequality of human capital accumulation over time. Considering endogenous fertility, as shown by Zhang (1997) and Yasuoka and Miyake (2014), subsidies for education investment raise the human capital accumulation of children. However, child allowances reduce the human capital accumulation of children due to the trade-off between the quality and quantity of children. The results obtained by these studies are derived from small open economies. However, some works, such as that of De la Croix and Doepke (2003), examine closed economy models.

The author would like to thank seminar participants for their helpful comments. Research for this paper was supported financially by JSPS KAKENHI Grant Numbers 17K03746 and 17K03791. Nevertheless, any remaining errors are the author's responsibility.

M. Yasuoka (✉)
School of Economics, Kwansei Gakuin University, Nishinomiya, Japan
e-mail: yasuoka@kwansei.ac.jp

M. Jinno and M. Yasuoka (eds.), *Fertility, Education and Macroeconomics: The Case of Japan*, https://doi.org/10.1007/978-981-95-1024-5_4

There is extensive literature on childcare policies within endogenous fertility models. However, few works examine these models with monetary assets. When considering a macroeconomic model with endogenous fertility, the monetary stock as an asset should be taken into account.

This chapter examines how monetary policy affects fertility and the income growth rate. If the inflation rate is altered by monetary policy, the physical capital stock changes as households adjust their asset allocation between real assets, such as physical capital investment, and nominal assets, such as money. Changes in the physical capital stock influence the wage rate and interest rate, thereby affecting childcare costs through either the cost of childcare services or opportunity costs. An increase in the money stock policy raises the inflation rate, decreasing the value of money as an asset. Consequently, the physical capital stock increases, leading to higher income growth rates. This increase in the physical capital stock raises childcare costs and boosts educational investment, enhancing the quality of children due to the substitution between the quality and quantity of children. This chapter considers human capital accumulation as a measure of children's quality and concludes that human capital accumulation is facilitated by the increased effects of monetary policy.

Many related works describe studies on money and inflation. Mino and Shibata (1995) explore how monetary policy affects income growth. The optimal monetary policy is derived by De Gregorio (1993) and Bhattacharya et al. (2009). Yasuoka (2018) demonstrates that the optimal monetary policy is influenced by the level of pay-as-you-go pensions. Yakita (2006) develops an endogenous growth model with monetary assets, showing that an increase in life expectancy affects the inflation rate and income growth rate. Fanti (2012) and Chang et al. (2013) incorporate monetary stock into an endogenous fertility model, finding that an increase in the money stock impacts fertility.

In this model, the inflation rate is determined by the rate of increase of the nominal monetary stock, fertility (population growth), and human capital growth (income growth). However, the effect of childcare policy on the inflation rate is generally ambiguous. For instance, a child allowance raises fertility but reduces human capital growth, which has opposing effects on the inflation rate.

The remainder of this chapter is organized as follows: Sect. 2 presents the model. Section 3 explains the derivation of the equilibrium. Section 4 examines how child allowances, education subsidies, and increases in the money stock policy affect fertility, the human capital growth rate (income growth rate), inflation, and the physical capital stock per unit of effective labor. The final section concludes the chapter.

2 Model

As described in this chapter, the model includes agents of three types: households, firms, and a government.

2.1 Household

Households in this model live through three periods: childhood, adulthood, and old age. In childhood, individuals receive education investment from their parents. In adulthood, individuals decide on the number of children n_t, the education investment for children e_t, the demand for real money stock per capita m_t, consumption in adulthood c_{1t}, and saving s_t for consumption in old age c_{2t+1}. Here, t denotes the period. For these analyses, we use a three-period overlapping generations model: in any period t, children, younger adults, and older adults all coexist. The budget constraint in adulthood is:

$$s_t = w_t h_t - c_{1t} - (z_t - q_t)n_t - (1 - x_t)e_t n_t - m_t - T_t. \tag{1}$$

In this equation, z_t denotes the childcare cost per child. The net childcare cost is given as $z_t - q_t$, where q_t denotes the child allowance. x_t represents the subsidy rate for education investment. w_t and h_t respectively denote the wage rate per unit of effective labor and the human capital stock. T_t stands for the lump sum tax used to fund childcare policies such as the child allowance q_t and the education subsidy x_t. In the old period, the budget constraint is given as

$$(1 + r_{t+1})s_t + \frac{m_t}{1 + \pi_{t+1}} + p_{t+1} = c_{2t+1}. \tag{2}$$

As shown here, r_{t+1} and π_{t+1} denote the real interest rate and the inflation rate. Considering (1) and (2), the lifetime budget constraint can be reduced.

$$\begin{aligned} w_t h_t - T_t = c_{1t} + \frac{c_{2t+1}}{1 + r_{t+1}} + (z_t - q_t)n_t + (1 - x_t)e_t n_t \\ + \left(1 - \frac{1}{(1 + r_{t+1})(1 + \pi_{t+1})}\right)m_t \end{aligned} \tag{3}$$

The human capital accumulation of children is formed by the following equation:

$$h_{t+1} = He_t^{\varepsilon} h_t^{1-\varepsilon}, \quad 0 < H, \quad 0 < \varepsilon < 1. \tag{4}$$

The utility function is assumed as[1]

$$u_t = \alpha \ln n_t h_{t+1} + (1 - \alpha)\ln m_t + \ln c_{1t} + \rho \ln c_{2t+1}, \quad 0 < \alpha < 1, \quad 0 < \rho < 1. \tag{5}$$

The optimal allocations to maximize utility (5) subject to the lifetime budget constraint (3) are expressed as follows:

[1] This paper assumes the money in the utility model as assumed by Sidrauski (1967), Yakita (2006), Walsh (2010), and others.

$$n_t = \frac{\alpha(1-\varepsilon)}{z_t - q_t}\frac{1}{2+\rho}(w_t h_t - T_t) \tag{6}$$

$$e_t = \frac{\varepsilon(z_t - q_t)}{(1-\varepsilon)(1-x_t)} \tag{7}$$

$$c_{1t} = \frac{1}{2+\rho}(w_t h_t - T_t) \tag{8}$$

$$c_{2t+1} = \frac{\rho(1+r_{t+1})}{2+\rho}(w_t h_t - T_t) \tag{9}$$

$$m_t = \frac{1-\alpha}{2+\rho}\frac{w_t h_t - T_t}{1 - \frac{1}{(1+r_{t+1})(1+\pi_{t+1})}} \tag{10}$$

2.2 Firms

Final goods are produced by inputting physical capital stock K_t. The effective labor $L_t = N_t h_t$. N_t denotes the population size of younger people in period t. Production function Y_t is assumed as follows:

$$Y_t = AK_t^{\theta} L_t^{1-\theta}, \quad 0 < A, \quad 0 < \theta < 1. \tag{11}$$

Assuming a perfectly competitive market, the wage rate and the interest rate are given by marginal productivity as

$$w_t = A(1-\theta)k_t^{\theta} \tag{12}$$

$$1 + r_t = A\theta k_t^{\theta-1} \tag{13}$$

where $k_t = \frac{K_t}{N_t h_t}$. For these analyses, we assume that the physical capital stock is fully depreciated in a single period.

2.3 Government

Government child care policies provide a child allowance and education subsidy. In addition to these policies, a pension benefit is provided for older people. We respectively consider a child allowance $q_t = \overline{q} w_t h_t$, and education subsidy $x_t = x$. Also $\overline{q}, x$ and τ are, respectively, constant over time. With a balanced budget, the government budget constraint is given as

$$T_t = \overline{q} w_t h_t + x e_t n_t. \tag{14}$$

3 Equilibrium

This section presents derivation of the equilibrium. This model includes the assumption of the childcare cost as $z_t = \overline{z} w_t h_t$. Also, $\overline{z}$ is constant over time.[2] Given h_t and K_t, the growth rate of human capital $1 + g_t$ is given as[3]

$$1 + g_t = \frac{h_{t+1}}{h_t} = H\left(\frac{\varepsilon(\overline{z} - \overline{q})}{(1-\varepsilon)(1-x)}\right)^{\varepsilon} \tag{15}$$

The inflation rate π_{t+1} is given by the following equation:

$$\frac{m_{t+1}}{m_t} = \frac{1+\mu}{(1+\pi_{t+1})n_t} \tag{16}$$

where μ represents the rate of increase of the aggregate nominal money stock.[4]

The capital market equilibrium condition is given as $K_{t+1} = N_t s_t$. Then, the following equation can be derived:

$$K_{t+1} = N_t \left(1 - \frac{1+\alpha}{2+\rho} - \frac{1-\alpha}{2+\rho} \frac{1}{1 - \frac{1}{(1+r_{t+1})(1+\pi_{t+1})}}\right)(w_t h_t - T_t). \tag{17}$$

Considering $k_t = \frac{K_t}{N_t h_t}$, the dynamics of k_t is given as

$$n_t(1 + g_t)k_{t+1} = \left(1 - \frac{1+\alpha}{2+\rho} - \frac{1-\alpha}{2+\rho} \frac{1}{1 - \frac{1}{(1+r_{t+1})(1+\pi_{t+1})}}\right)\left(w_t - \frac{T_t}{h_t}\right). \tag{18}$$

Considering (6)–(10), (12)–(18), one obtains $c_{1t}, c_{2t+1}, n_t, e_t, m_t, w_t, r_{t+1}, g_t, \pi_{t+1}, k_{t+1}$ for given k_t.

The balanced growth path can be given as $k_{t+1} = k_t = k$. Then, the growth rate of human capital g_t is constant rate g. Without policy parameters, that is, $\overline{q} = 0$ and $x = 0$, the growth rate of human capital in the balanced growth path is given as

[2] This chapter assumes that the childcare cost is proportional to the wage rate. This is a consistent assumption because childcare services are provided by childcare labor, and the wage rate represents the cost of providing childcare. Yasuoka and Miyake (2010) explicitly consider the labor market for childcare services and derive that childcare service costs depend on the wage rate.

[3] The growth rate of human capital coincides with the income growth rate.

[4] Defining P_t as the price level and M_t as the aggregate nominal money stock, respectively, we obtain $m_t = \frac{M_t}{N_t P_t}$.

$$1 + g = H\left(\frac{\varepsilon\bar{z}w}{1-\varepsilon}\right)^{\varepsilon} \tag{19}$$

where

$$w = A(1-\theta)k^{\theta}. \tag{20}$$

In the balanced growth path, $\frac{m_{t+1}}{m_t} = 1 + g$ holds. Considering (16), the inflation rate in the balanced growth path π is

$$1 + \pi = \frac{1+\mu}{(1+g)n} \tag{21}$$

where

$$n = \frac{\alpha(1-\varepsilon)}{\bar{z}}\frac{1}{2+\rho}. \tag{22}$$

The interest rate in the balanced growth path is given as follows:

$$1 + r = A\theta k^{\theta-1} \tag{23}$$

Substituting (19)–(23) into (18), the capital stock per unit of effective unit of labor can be derived such that the following equation holds[5]:

$$\frac{\alpha H(1-\varepsilon)}{(2+\rho)\bar{z}^{1-\varepsilon}A^{1-\varepsilon}(1-\theta)^{1-\varepsilon}}\left(\frac{\varepsilon}{1-\varepsilon}\right)^{\varepsilon}k^{1-\theta(1-\varepsilon)} = 1 - \frac{1+\alpha}{2+\rho} - \frac{1-\alpha}{2+\rho}\frac{1}{1-\frac{\frac{\alpha H(1-\varepsilon)}{(2+\rho)\bar{z}^{1-\varepsilon}}\left(\frac{\varepsilon A(1-\theta)}{1-\varepsilon}\right)^{\varepsilon}k^{1-\theta(1-\varepsilon)}}{A\theta(1+\mu)}} \tag{24}$$

Considering (19)–(24), we obtain w, r, g, π, k, n in the balanced growth path.

4 Policy Effect

This section examines how policies such as an increase in money stock, child allowance, education subsidy, and pension benefit affect the income growth rate, fertility, and inflation.

[5] See the Appendix for the detailed proof of the local stability condition.

4.1 Increase in the Money Stock

This subsection examines the effect of an increase in money stock on the income growth rate, inflation rate, and other factors.

Defining the left-hand side of (24) as L and the right-hand side of (24) as R, respectively, one can obtain the unique steady state as shown in Fig. 1.

R shifts up and the physical capital stock per unit of effective labor increases because the intersection moves to the right if the rate of an increase in aggregate nominal money stock μ rises as the monetary policy. Then, with (19) and (20), the human capital growth rate or income growth rate g rises. However, the effect on the inflation rate is ambiguous.

Substituting (19), (20), and (22) into (21), with total differentiation with respect to π, μ, k, one obtains $\frac{d\pi}{d\mu}$ as

$$\frac{d\pi}{d\mu} = \frac{1}{n(1+g)}\left(1 - \frac{\varepsilon\theta(1+\mu)}{k}\right) \tag{25}$$

With $k > \varepsilon\theta(1+\mu)$, one can obtain $\frac{d\pi}{d\mu} > 0$: that is, an increase in money stock policy raises the inflation rate. Consequently, the following proposition can be established.

Proposition 1 If the rate of an increase in aggregate money stock rises, then the growth rate of human capital and the physical capital stock per unit of effective labor increase. The inflation rate increases if $k > \varepsilon\theta(1+\mu)$.

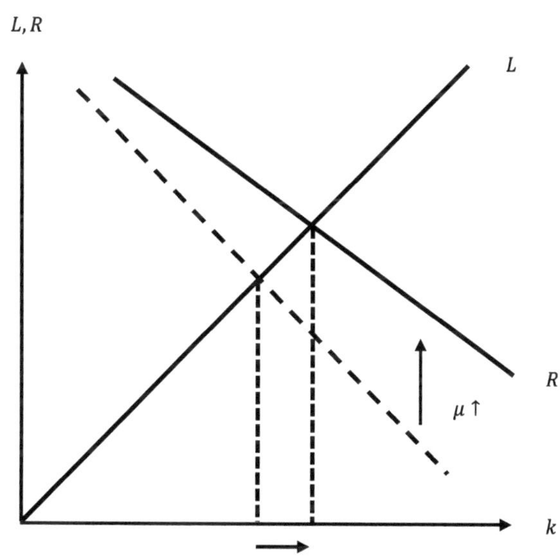

Fig. 1 Effect of k of an increase in μ

With an increase in money stock, the education investment for children increases because an increase in the wage rate caused by an increase in capital stock per unit of effective labor raises the cost to increase the number of children. As a result, because of substitution between the quality of children and the quantity of children, education investment increases and the human capital growth rate or income growth rate increases. In this policy, fertility does not change because both the child care cost and wage income increase. These increases are cancelled out.

4.2 Child Allowance

This subsection presents an examination of the child allowance effect. Then, the government budget constraint (14) changes to the following equation:

$$T_t = \overline{q} w_t h_t \tag{26}$$

Considering (6) and (26), we obtain the following fertility. An increase in child allowance level $\overline{q}$ raises fertility.

$$n = \frac{\frac{\alpha(1-\varepsilon)}{2+\rho}}{\overline{z} - \left(1 - \frac{\alpha(1-\varepsilon)}{2+\rho}\right)\overline{q}} \tag{27}$$

With total differentiation of (15) with respect to $g, \overline{q}, k$, one obtains the following:

$$\frac{dg}{d\overline{q}} = -\frac{\varepsilon(1+g)}{\overline{z}} + \frac{\varepsilon\theta(1+g)}{k}\frac{dk}{d\overline{q}}. \tag{28}$$

The physical capital stock is given such that the following equation holds:

$$n(1+g)k = \left(1 - \frac{1+\alpha}{2+\rho} - \frac{1-\alpha}{2+\rho}\frac{1}{1-\frac{1}{(1+r)(1+\pi)}}\right)(1-\overline{q}n)w. \tag{29}$$

Regarding the variables therein, $1+g, w, 1+\pi, 1+r, n$ are given respectively as (15), (20), (21), (23), and (27). From total differentiation of (15), (20), (21), (23), (27), and (29) with respect to $k, 1+g, w, 1+\pi, 1+r, n, \overline{q}$, one can obtain $\frac{dk}{d\overline{q}}$ as[6]

$$\frac{dk}{d\overline{q}} = -\frac{n\left(\left(1 - \frac{\alpha(1-\varepsilon)}{2+\rho} - \varepsilon\right)\frac{1+g}{\overline{z}}\left(\frac{k}{w} + \frac{(1-\alpha)\left(1-\frac{n(1+g)}{(1+r)(1+\mu)}\right)^{-2}}{(2+\rho)(1+\mu)(1+r)}\right) + \left(1 - \frac{1+\alpha}{2+\rho} - \frac{1-\alpha}{2+\rho}\frac{1}{1-\frac{1}{(1+r)(1+\pi)}}\right)\right)}{X_1} \tag{30}$$

[6] See the Appendix for total differentiation.

where

$$X_1 = n(1+g)(1-\theta(1-\varepsilon))\left(\frac{1}{w} + \frac{1-\alpha}{(2+\rho)(1+\mu)A\theta k^{\theta}}\right)$$
$$\left(1 - \frac{n(1+g)}{(1+r)(1+\mu)}\right)^{-2} \tag{31}$$

The sign of $\frac{dk}{d\overline{q}}$ is always negative $\frac{dk}{d\overline{q}} < 0$. The child allowance reduces the capital stock per unit of effective labor. Because of $\frac{dk}{d\overline{q}}$, one can obtain $\frac{dg}{d\overline{q}} < 0$.

From (21), the effects on the inflation rate are

$$\frac{d\pi}{d\overline{q}} = (1+\pi)\left(\frac{-\left(1 - \frac{\alpha(1-\varepsilon)}{2+\rho}\right) + \varepsilon}{\overline{z}} - \frac{\varepsilon\theta}{k}\frac{dk}{d\overline{q}}\right) \tag{32}$$

The sign of $\frac{d\pi}{d\overline{q}}$ is ambiguous. The child allowance increases fertility, which reduces the inflation rate. The term of $\frac{\varepsilon}{\overline{z}} - \frac{\varepsilon\theta}{k}\frac{dk}{d\overline{q}}$ shows the positive effect on the inflation rate via the change of the human capital growth rate. Consequently, the following proposition can be established.

Proposition 2 The child allowance can raise fertility and reduce the capital stock per unit of effective labor and the human capital growth rate. The inflation rate effect is ambiguous.

Basically, this proposition does not significantly differ from the findings of previous studies. Child allowance increases the number of children, as shown in the results obtained by van Groezen et al. (2003) and Yasuoka and Goto (2011). Similarly, the finding that it reduces the accumulation of human capital, as observed by Zhang (1997), is also confirmed.

4.3 Education Subsidy

This subsection presents derivation of how the education subsidy affects the capital stock per unit of effective labor, the human capital growth rate, fertility, and the inflation rate. The government budget constraint (14) is given by the following:

$$T_t = xe_t n_t = \frac{x\varepsilon\overline{z}wh_t}{(1-\varepsilon)(1-x)}. \tag{33}$$

Then, the fertility is given as

$$n = \frac{\alpha(1-\varepsilon)}{\bar{z}(2+\rho)\left(1+\frac{\alpha\varepsilon x}{(2+\rho)(1-x)}\right)} \tag{34}$$

Therefore, we obtain $\frac{dn}{dx} < 0$, i.e., the education subsidy decreases fertility.

Substituting (33) into (18) and performing total differentiation with respect to x, k at the approximation of $x = 0$, one obtains $\frac{dn}{dx}$. The numerator of $\frac{dk}{dx}$ is[7]

$$\frac{dk}{dx} = \frac{X_2}{X_1} < 0, \tag{35}$$

where

$$X_2 = -\left(1-\frac{\alpha}{2+\rho}\right)\left(\frac{1-\alpha}{(2+\rho)(1+r)(1+\mu)}\left(1-\frac{1}{(1+r)(1+\pi)}\right)^{-2}+\frac{k}{w}\right)\varepsilon n(1+g)-\frac{\alpha\varepsilon}{2+\rho}$$
$$\left(1-\frac{1+\alpha}{2+\rho}-\frac{1-\alpha}{2+\rho}\frac{1}{1-\frac{1}{(1+r)(1+\pi)}}\right)<0. \tag{36}$$

Then, the sign of (36) is negative. The subsidy for education investment reduces the physical capital stock per unit of effective labor. Then, human capital accumulation does not always increase because

$$\frac{dg}{dx} = \varepsilon(1+g)\left(\frac{\theta}{k}\frac{dk}{dx}+1\right). \tag{37}$$

Because of $\frac{dk}{dx} < 0$, the sign of (37) is ambiguous even if the subsidy for education investment has a direct positive effect on the human capital growth rate. Moreover, the effect on the inflation rate is ambiguous because

$$\frac{d\pi}{dx} = \varepsilon(1+g)\left(\frac{\alpha}{2+\rho}-\frac{\theta}{k}\frac{dk}{dx}-1\right). \tag{38}$$

The decrease in fertility raises the inflation rate, as shown by the first term. The second and third terms represent the effect of income growth on the inflation rate. An increase in the income growth rate reduces the inflation rate. However, because $\frac{dk}{dx} < 0$, the negative effect of income growth rate on the inflation rate is weakened. Then, the following proposition can be established.

Proposition 3 The subsidy for education decreases fertility. The physical capital stock per unit of effective labor decreases. Therefore, because $\frac{dk}{dx} < 0$, the subsidy for education investment can not always raise the human capital growth rate. The effect on the inflation rate is ambiguous.

[7] See the Appendix for total differentiation.

This proposition yields results almost identical to those of Zhang (1997). While subsidies for education promote the accumulation of human capital, they also lead to a reduction in the number of children.

5 Conclusions

In a model where fertility is endogenized, the significance of considering a model of holding money can be explained as follows. There are two types of asset holdings: holding money and holding physical capital stock. Essentially, individuals will choose to hold the asset that yields a higher return. As a result, when the nominal money supply increases and subsequently the inflation rate rises, the return on real assets like physical capital stock becomes relatively higher. Consequently, households will prefer to hold capital stock. Unlike money, physical capital stock affects interest rates and wage rates, thereby influencing household income. This change in household income due to the effects of monetary policy has the potential to alter the number of children and investment in education. Therefore, this study is considered significant.

Regarding child allowances and educational subsidies, the results did not differ significantly from those of previous studies. In other words, child allowances increase the number of children but suppress the accumulation of human capital, while educational subsidies decrease the number of children but promote the accumulation of human capital.

On the other hand, a policy that increases the money supply has the effect of raising the physical capital stock. However, in this model, child care costs are also proportional to wages, so even if household income increases due to an increase in physical capital stock, the number of children does not change. On the other hand, investment in education increases, thereby promoting the accumulation of human capital.

Previous studies have shown that educational subsidy policies have the effect of lowering the number of children. However, policies that increase the money supply have the effect of promoting the accumulation of human capital without lowering the number of children. Considering that educational subsidy policies lower the number of children more, it can be said that policies that increase the money supply, which promote the accumulation of human capital without lowering the number of children, are desirable.

Appendix

Dynamics of k

Total differentiation of (18) with respect to k_t and k_{t+1} at the balanced growth path without policy is given as

$$\frac{dk_{t+1}}{dk_t} = \frac{n(1+g)\theta(1-\varepsilon) - \frac{(1-\alpha)n(1+g)(1-\theta)}{(2+\rho)(1+\mu)A\theta k^{\theta}}\left(1 - \frac{1}{(1+r)(1+\pi)}\right)^{-2}}{n(1+g) + \frac{(1-\alpha)n(1+g)(1-\theta)}{(2+\rho)(1+\mu)A\theta k^{\theta}}\left(1 - \frac{1}{(1+r)(1+\pi)}\right)^{-2}}. \tag{39}$$

With $-1 < \frac{dk_{t+1}}{dk_t} < 1$, the balanced growth path is locally stable.
Derivation of $\frac{dk}{d\overline{q}}$
From (27), one can obtain

$$dn = \frac{\left(1 - \frac{\alpha(1-\epsilon)}{2+\rho}\right)n}{\overline{z}} d\overline{q}. \tag{40}$$

Considering (20), (21), (23), (28), and (40), the left-hand side of (29) is changed by total differentiation as

$$\frac{(1+g)nk}{w\overline{z}}\left(1 - \frac{\alpha(1-\epsilon)}{2+\rho} - \epsilon\right)d\overline{q} + \frac{n(1+g)(1-\theta(1-\epsilon))}{w}dk. \tag{41}$$

Total differentiation of the right-hand side of (29) is reduced to the following:

$$-\frac{(1-\alpha)\alpha(1-\epsilon)}{(2+\rho)^2(1+\mu)A\theta}\left(1 - \frac{n(1+g)}{(1+r)(1+\pi)}\right)^{-2}$$
$$\left(\frac{(1-\theta(1-\epsilon))(1+g)k^{-\theta}}{\overline{z}}dk + \frac{(1+g)k^{1-\theta}}{\overline{z}^2}\left(1 - \frac{\alpha(1-\epsilon)}{2+\rho} - \epsilon\right)d\overline{q}\right)$$
$$+n\left(1 - \frac{1+\alpha}{(2+\rho)} - \frac{1-\alpha}{2+\rho}\frac{1}{1 - \frac{1}{(1+r)(1+\pi)}}\right)d\overline{q}. \tag{42}$$

From (41) and (42), one can obtain $\frac{dk}{d\overline{q}}$.
Derivation of $\frac{dk}{dx}$
From (34), one can obtain the following:

$$dn = -\frac{\alpha\epsilon n}{(2+\rho)}dx = -\frac{\alpha^2\epsilon(1-\epsilon)}{\overline{z}(2+\rho)^2}dx. \tag{43}$$

Considering (15), (18), (20), (21), (23), (33), and (43), the left-hand side of (18) is changed by the total differentiation at the approximation of $T_t = 0$ with respect to x, k as

$$\frac{\epsilon(1+g)nk}{w}\left(1-\frac{\alpha}{2+\rho}\right)dx+\frac{n(1+g)(1-\theta(1-\epsilon))}{w}dk. \tag{44}$$

Total differentiation of the right-hand side of (18) is reduced to

$$-\frac{(1-\alpha)\alpha(1-\epsilon)n(1+g)}{(2+\rho)(1+\mu)}\left(1-\frac{n(1+g)}{(1+r)(1+\pi)}\right)^{-2}$$
$$\left(\frac{1-\theta(1-\varepsilon)}{A\theta k^{\theta}}dk+\frac{\varepsilon}{1+r}\left(1-\frac{\alpha}{2+\rho}\right)dx\right)$$
$$-\frac{\alpha\epsilon}{2+\rho}\left(1-\frac{\alpha}{(2+\rho)}-\frac{1-\alpha}{2+\rho}\frac{1}{1-\frac{1}{(1+r)(1+\pi)}}\right)dx. \tag{45}$$

From (44) and (45), one can obtain $\frac{dk}{dx}$.

References

Bhattacharya, J., Haslag, J., and Martin, A. (2009). Optimal monetary policy and economic growth. *European Economic Review, 53*, 210–21.

Chang, W., Chen, Y., and Chang, J. (2013). Growth and welfare effects of monetary policy with endogenous fertility. *Journal of Macroeconomics, 35*, 117–30.

De Gregorio, J. (1993) Inflation, taxation, and long-run growth. *Journal of Monetary Economics, 31*, 271–98.

De la Croix, D., and Doepke, M. (2003). Inequality and growth: Why differential fertility matters. *American Economic Review, 93*(4), 1091–13.

Fanti, L. (2012). *Fertility and money in an OLG model.* Discussion Papers 2012/145, Dipartimento di Economia e Management (DEM), University of Pisa, Pisa, Italy.

Fanti, L., and Gori, L. (2009). Population and neoclassical economic growth: A new child policy perspective. *Economics Letters, 104*(1), 27–30.

Glomm, G., and Ravikumar, B. (1992). Public versus private investment in human capital endogenous growth and income inequality. *Journal of Political Economy, 100*(4), 818–34.

Mino, K., and Shibata, A. (1995). Monetary policy, overlapping generations, and patterns of growth. *Economica, 62*, 179–94.

Miyazaki, K. (2013). Pay-as-you-go social security and endogenous fertility in a neoclassical growth model. *Journal of Population Economics, 26*(3), 1233–50.

Sidrauski, M. (1967). Rational choice and patterns of growth in a monetary economy. *American Economic Review, 57*, 534–44.

Van Groezen, B., Leers, T. and Meijdam, L. (2003). Social security and endogenous fertility: Pensions and child allowances as Siamese twins. *Journal of Public Economics, 87*(2), 233–51.

Van Groezen, B., and Meijdam, L. (2008). Growing old and staying young: Population policy in an ageing closed economy. *Journal of Population Economics, 21*(3), 573–88.

Walsh, C. (2010). *Monetary theory and policy*, Third ed. MIT Press.

Yakita, A. (2006). Life expectancy, money, and growth. *Journal of Population Economics, 19*(3), 579–92.

Yasuoka, M. (2018), Money and pay-as-you-go pension. *Economies, 6*(2), 1–15.

Yasuoka, M., and Goto, N. (2011). Pension and child care policies with endogenous fertility. *Economic Modelling, 28*(6), 2478–82.

Yasuoka, M., and Goto, N. (2015). How is the child allowance to be financed? By income tax or consumption tax? *International Review of Economics, 62*(3), 249–69.

Yasuoka, M., and Miyake, A. (2010). Change in the transition of the fertility rate. *Economics Letters, 106*(2), 78–80.

Yasuoka, M., and Miyake, A. (2014). Fertility rate and child care policies in a pension system. *Economic Analysis and Policy, 44*(1), 122–27.

Zhang, J. (1997). Fertility, growth, and public investments in children. *Canadian Journal of Economics, 30*(4), 835–43.

Masaya Yasuoka is a professor at the School of Economics, Kwansei Gakuin University. His main areas of research interest are public finance, social security, and macroeconomics. He has published papers in scholarly journals including *Economics Letters, Economic Modelling, International Review of Economics* and *Journal of the Economics of Ageing*. Professor Yasuoka received a B.A. in economics from Nagoya City University and a Ph.D. in economics from Kobe University.

Chapter 5
Fertility and Labor Share of Child Care Service

Masaya Shintani and Masaya Yasuoka

1 Introduction

Our chapter examines how preferences for rearing children affect fertility in the endogenous child care service price. The preference for rearing children is related to life expectancy. An increase in life expectancy reduces the preference for rearing children. Thereby, fertility decreases. This result was derived from the work of Yakita (2001), van Groezen, Leers, and Meijdam (2003), and others as reported in the related literature. However, the relative decrease in the preference for rearing children with an increase in life expectancy raises the preference for consumption in the old period. Consequently, the saving rate increases. Then, the capital accumulation is facilitated. Further, the capital stock per capita increases because of increased savings and decreased fertility.

The aim of this chapter is to examine how fertility is determined in an endogenous fertility model with a child care services sector. Our works sets a two-sector model, with a final goods sector and a child care service sector, based on Yasuoka (2020).[1] From the endogenous prices of child care services, our manuscript derives the result that an increased preference for children cannot always raise fertility. Therefore,

[1] Yasuoka (2020) sets a two-sector model: a final goods sector and an elderly care service sector. However, Yasuoka (2020) also considers a small open economy without consideration of capital accumulation.

Research for this paper was supported financially by JSPS KAKENHI No.17 K03746 and No.17 K03791. Nevertheless, any remaining errors are the authors' responsibility.

M. Shintani (✉)
Faculty of Economics, Hiroshima University of Economics, Hiroshima, Japan
e-mail: ms-shinta@hue.ac.jp

M. Yasuoka
School of Economics, Kwansei Gakuin University, Nishinomiya, Japan
e-mail: yasuoka@kwansei.ac.jp

M. Jinno and M. Yasuoka (eds.), *Fertility, Education and Macroeconomics: The Case of Japan*, https://doi.org/10.1007/978-981-95-1024-5_5

a decrease in the preference for rearing children as an increase in life expectancy cannot always reduce fertility. If the demand for child care decreases, the price of child care services reduces due to this decrease in demand. A decrease in demand for child care services results in an increase in such services, which in turn leads to a rise in fertility. This result differs from those in reports of the related literature in that a decrease in the preference for rearing children by an increase in life expectancy reduces the fertility.

Moreover, we verify the effects of a child care service subsidy on fertility. Because of the subsidy, both the share of those using child care services and the labor share of the child care services sector increases. Then, the wage rate of the child care services sector rises. As a result, we can obtain positive correlation between fertility and labor force participation. This result is consistent with data provided by Sleebos (2003).

Apps and Rees (2004) and Ferrero and Iza (2004) consider child care services and parental child care time. They identify correlation between the fertility and female labor participation, which a positive relationship. If one considers only parental child care, then negative correlation is obtainable, as shown by Galor and Weil (1996). By virtue of capital accumulation, the demand for child care services increases and the child care time decreases. The mentioned works in this section describe that fertility is positively correlated with female labor force participation. Unlike the results obtained in this literature, we examine how the subsidy for child care services affects the share of individuals using such services and the labor share of the child care services sector.

Van Groezen, Leers, and Meijdam (2003) show that the child allowance, as a subsidy for child care, raises fertility. However, if one considers capital accumulation, then the child allowance reduces fertility, as explained by Fanti and Gori (2009), because a decrease in capital accumulation reduces the wage income. Yasuoka and Miyake (2010) present the negative effect of subsidy policy on fertility because of an increase in child care services.

The remaining parts of this chapter present our examination and its salient conclusions. Section 2 sets the model. Section 3 identifies the equilibrium and examines how the preference for children affects fertility. Section 4 examines effects of a subsidy for child care services on fertility and income growth. Section 5 discusses the results obtained in our work. The final section concludes the chapter.

2 Model

Individuals in households live in two periods: young and old. During the young period, the children work to obtain income. They then consume goods in the old period.

We assume the following log utility function:

$$u_t = \alpha \ln n_t + (1-\alpha) \ln c_{t+1}, 0 < \alpha < 1. \tag{1}$$

In this equation, n_t and c_{t+1} denote fertility (number of children) and consumption in the old period. In this model, two types of child care exist: self-child care, representing parental time spent, and purchased child care services provided through the child care services market. If the individuals use the child care service, then the lifetime budget

$$\overline{w}_t = z_t n_t + \frac{c_{t+1}}{1 + r_{t+1}}. \tag{2}$$

In that equation, $\overline{w}_t$ represents the wage income, z_t denotes the price of child care. services, and r_{t+1} denotes the interest rate. Therefore, the parents use the child care services; they can provide a full-time supply of labor.

If the individuals care for the children by themselves, then the budget constraint is

$$(1 - \phi n_t)\overline{w}_t = \frac{c_{t+1}}{1 + r_{t+1}} \tag{3}$$

In that equation, ϕ is needed for the care time for a child. Because of the child care time ϕn_t, the parents supply labor time of $1 - \phi n_t$.

Two types of firms of exist in this model economy: one produces final goods; the other produces child care services. The production function in the firm producing final goods is assumed as

$$Y_t = K_t^{\theta}(B_t L_t)^{1-\theta}, 0 < \theta < 1. \tag{4}$$

The output of final goods Y_t is produced by inputting the capital stock K_t and the effective labor L_t. $B_t = b\frac{K_t}{L_t}$ $(b > 0)$ shows the Romer (1986) and Grossman and Yanagawa (1993) type of externality. With a competitive market, the effective wage rate w_t and the interest rate $1 + r_t$ are given by the following:

$$w_t = (1 - \theta)b^{1-\theta}\frac{K_t}{L_t}, \tag{5}$$

$$1 + r_t = \theta b^{1-\theta} \tag{6}$$

The profit function π_t in the child care service is assumed as

$$\pi_t = z_t \rho L_t^c - w_t^c L_t^c, 0 < \rho. \tag{7}$$

Therein, L_t^c represents the labor input to child care services. Also, w_t^c denotes the wage rate in child care services. With a competitive market, the wage rate in the child care service sector is shown as presented below:

$$z_t = \frac{w_t^c}{\rho} \tag{8}$$

As described in this chapter, we assume that individuals have ability a. This ability a is assumed to differ among individuals; it is distributed in $[0, \overline{a}]$. This ability a shows labor productivity in the production of the final goods. If individuals work in the final goods market, they can obtain $\overline{w}_t = aw_t$. If they work in the child care market, they can obtain $\overline{w}_t = w_t^c$, irrespective of a. This setting is based on the explanation presented by Meckl and Zink (2004).[2] Therefore, with high a, they work in the final goods sector. Otherwise, they work in the child care service sector.[3] The cutoff ability $\tilde{a}$ is given as

$$\tilde{a} = \frac{w_t^c}{w_t}. \tag{9}$$

Then, the labor shares of the child care service sector and the final goods sector are shown respectively by $\frac{\tilde{a}}{\overline{a}}$ and $\frac{\overline{a}-\tilde{a}}{\overline{a}}$.

If the workers in the final goods sector use child care services, their fertility is shown as[4]

$$n_t = \frac{\alpha a w_t}{z_t}. \tag{10}$$

If care time for children is given without child care service, then the fertility can be presented as[5]

$$n_t = \frac{\alpha a w_t}{\phi a w_t} = \frac{\alpha}{\phi}. \tag{11}$$

We define the ability a to hold $\frac{\alpha a w_t}{z_t} = \frac{\alpha}{\phi}$ as $\hat{a}$. $\hat{a}$ shows indifference between child care by the market service and that by one's own time. If individuals have ability $a > \hat{a}$, they use the child care service. Otherwise, they care for children using their own time. Therefore, the share of $\frac{\overline{a}-\hat{a}}{\overline{a}}$ uses the child care service. Considering (8)–(11), the following equation can be obtained:

$$\hat{a} = \frac{\tilde{a}}{\phi\rho}. \tag{12}$$

We assume $\phi\rho < 1$ for simplicity. Then, we can obtain $\hat{a} > \tilde{a}$. Therefore, individuals with ability $[0, \tilde{a}]$ work in the child care services sector and care for their children using their own time. Individuals who have ability $[\tilde{a}, \hat{a}]$ work in the final

[2] Meckl and Zink (2004) consider labor of two types: skilled and unskilled. Skilled laborers obtain $a^2 w_t$. By contrast, unskilled laborers obtain awt. Substantially, this setting is the same as that used for the analyses presented herein.

[3] Productivity a shows no absolute ability of labor but a relative ability. Low a shows insufficient skill in the final goods sector but high skill in the child goods sector.

[4] We can obtain fertility to maximize utility (1) subject to (2).

[5] We can obtain fertility to maximize utility (1) subject to (3). The fertility of child care service workers can be given as (11).

goods sector and care for their children using their own time. Individuals who have ability $[\widehat{a}, \overline{a}]$ work in the final goods sector and use the child care services for their children.

3 Equilibrium

This section presents the derivation of the equilibrium of the model economy. The equilibrium can be given by the child care services market and the capital market. First, we consider the child care market equilibrium. Demand for child care services is given as $\int_{\widehat{a}}^{\overline{a}} \frac{\alpha a w_t}{z_t} \frac{1}{\overline{a}} da$. The supply for child care services is given as (9). Then, because of these two equations, the following equation can be shown as the child care services market equilibrium condition:

$$\frac{\alpha\left(\overline{a}^2 - \widehat{a}^2\right)}{2\phi\widehat{a}} = \tilde{a}. \tag{13}$$

With (12) and (13), we can obtain $\widehat{a}$ and $\tilde{a}$

$$\widehat{a} = \overline{a}\sqrt{\frac{\alpha}{2\phi^2\rho + \alpha}}, \tag{14}$$

$$\tilde{a} = \phi\rho\overline{a}\sqrt{\frac{\alpha}{2\phi^2\rho + \alpha}} \tag{15}$$

After obtaining $\frac{d\widehat{a}}{d\alpha} > 0$, $\frac{d\widehat{a}}{d\phi} < 0$, $\frac{d\widehat{a}}{d\rho} < 0$ and $\frac{d\tilde{a}}{d\alpha} > 0$, $\frac{d\tilde{a}}{d\phi} < 0$, $\frac{d\tilde{a}}{d\rho} < 0$, one can consider a decrease in the preference for children α as representing the case of an aging society with fewer children. A decrease in α decreases $\widehat{a}$: the share of using child care services increases because the number of children at each household decreases.

The average number of children or fertility n^a is given as

$$n^a = \int_{\widehat{a}}^{a} \frac{\alpha a w_t}{z_t} \frac{1}{\overline{a}} da + \int_0^{\widehat{a}} \frac{\alpha}{\phi} \frac{1}{\overline{a}} da \tag{16}$$

The sign of $\frac{dn^a}{d\alpha}$ is ambiguous because

$$\frac{dn^a}{d\alpha} = \frac{n^a}{\alpha} - \frac{\alpha\left(\frac{\overline{a}^2}{\widehat{a}^2} - 1\right)}{2\phi\overline{a}} \frac{d\widehat{a}}{d\alpha} \tag{17}$$

The sign of $\frac{dn^a}{d\alpha}$ is determined depending on the level of n^a. Large n^a brings about $\frac{dn^a}{d\alpha} > 0$. However, with small n^a, we can obtain $\frac{dn^a}{d\alpha} < 0$: even if the preference for children increases, the fertility cannot always increase because of the child care services market. As shown by (10) and (11), an increase in α raises fertility. However, with an increase in the demand for child care services, the prices of child care services rise, which reduces the demand for child care services. This, in turn, reduces fertility. The former positive effect and the latter negative effect on fertility coexist; therefore, the overall effect on fertility is ambiguous. The following proposition can be established.

Proposition 1 *An increase in the preference for children α cannnot always raise fertility. An increase in the preference for children α raises $\hat{a}$.*

If we consider the model economy without child care services or a one-sector model, then fertility can always be raised by virtue of an increase in α. However, by considering child care services as a two-sector model, an increase in α does not always raise fertility.

Next, we examine the effects of a preference for children α on income growth. Defining $k_t = \frac{K_t}{N_t}$ (N_t denotes the population size of younger people) as the capital stock per capita and $L_t = \left(\frac{\overline{a}-\hat{a}}{\overline{a}} + \frac{\left(\hat{a}-\tilde{a}\right)(1-\phi n)}{\overline{a}}\right)N_t$ as effective labor, the capital market equilibrium is given as[6]

$$K_{t+1} = N_t(1-\alpha)\left(\int_{\tilde{a}}^{\overline{a}} aw_t\frac{1}{\overline{a}}da + \int_0^{\tilde{a}} w_t^c\frac{1}{\overline{a}}da\right) = \frac{1-\alpha}{\overline{a}}\frac{\overline{a}^2+\hat{a}^2}{2}w_t \tag{18}$$

Then, the income growth rate $1+g \equiv \frac{k_{t+1}}{k_t}$ is given as

$$\frac{k_{t+1}}{k_t} = \frac{(1-\alpha)(1-\theta)b^{1-\theta}\left(\overline{a}^2+\phi^2\rho^2\hat{a}^2\right)}{2n^a\left(\overline{a}-(1-(1-\rho\phi)(1-\alpha))\hat{a}\right)} \tag{19}$$

As shown by (19), an increase in the preference for children α reduces the income growth rate directly because saving for consumption in the old period decreases. However, an increase in α raises $\hat{a}$. This effect raises the income growth rate. Moreover, an increase in α reduces L_t, which positively affects income growth. If the average fertility n^a increases, then this effect on the income growth rate is negative because of the dilutive effect on the capital stock. Therefore, the increase in effects on income growth is ambiguous because these effects exist. In turn, the following proposition can be established.

Proposition 2 *An increase in α cannot always reduce income growth rate because of ambiguous effects on average fertility and positive effects on $\hat{a}$.*

[6] L_t Denotes the labor input for final goods sector. Therefore, workers of the child care services sector are not included.

As shown by the related literature, an increase in life expectancy, which entails a decrease in the preference for children, raises the income growth rate because saving increases and fertility decreases. However, if we regard the prices of child care services as a two-sector model, the income growth rate cannot always increase because fertility can decrease and $\hat{a}$ increases. An increase in $\hat{a}$ increases $\tilde{a}$, as shown by (12). The wage income of the child care service workers increases and saving increases. Therefore, these counter-effects exist. The effect of an increase in preference for children on income growth is ambiguous.

4 Subsidy for Child Care Service

This section examines the effects of a subsidy for child care services on fertility. Defining ε and τ respectively as the subsidy rate of child care service and the income tax rate, household budget constraints (2) and (3) are changed as shown below:

$$(1-\tau)\overline{w}_t = (1-\varepsilon)z_t n_t + \frac{c_{t+1}}{1+r_{t+1}}. \tag{20}$$

$$(1-\phi n_t)(1-\tau)\overline{w}_t = \frac{c_{t+1}}{1+r_{t+1}} \tag{21}$$

The government budget constraint is given as

$$\varepsilon\int_{\hat{a}}^{\overline{a}} z_t n_t \frac{1}{\overline{a}}da = \tau\left(\int_{\hat{a}}^{\overline{a}} a w_t \frac{1}{\overline{a}}da + \int_{\tilde{a}}^{\hat{a}}(1-\phi n)a w_t\frac{1}{\overline{a}}da + \int_0^{\tilde{a}}(1-\phi n)w_t^c\frac{1}{\overline{a}}da\right) \tag{22}$$

In this case, $\tilde{a}$ is given as (9). Also, $\hat{a}$ is shown as

$$\hat{a} = \frac{(1-\varepsilon)\tilde{a}}{(1-\tau)\phi\rho} \tag{23}$$

By total differentiation of (22) and (23) with respect to $\varepsilon, \tau, \hat{a}$, and $\tilde{a}$ at the approximation of $\varepsilon = 0$ and $\tau = 0$, one can obtain the following equation:

$$d\varepsilon = \frac{\overline{a}^2 - \alpha\hat{a}^2 + (1-\alpha)\tilde{a}^2}{\alpha\left(\overline{a}^2 - \hat{a}^2\right)}, \tag{24}$$

$$d\hat{a} = \hat{a}d\tau - \frac{\tilde{a}}{\phi\rho}d\varepsilon + \frac{1}{\phi\rho}d\tilde{a}. \tag{25}$$

The child care service market equilibrium (13) is modified as the following form in the case of a subsidy:

$$\frac{\alpha w_t(1-\tau)}{(1-\varepsilon)z_t}\frac{\overline{a}^2-\widehat{a}^2}{2}=\rho\tilde{a} \tag{26}$$

Considering $\frac{(1-\tau)w_t}{(1-\varepsilon)z_t}=\frac{1}{\widehat{a}\phi}$ and total differentiation of this equation with respect to $\widehat{a}$, $\tilde{a}$, we can obtain

$$d\widehat{a}=-\frac{\phi\rho\widehat{a}}{\alpha\widehat{a}+\phi\rho\tilde{a}}d\tilde{a}. \tag{27}$$

With (24), (25) and (27), we can obtain $\frac{d\widehat{a}}{d\tau}$ as shown below:

$$\frac{d\widehat{a}}{d\tau}=\frac{\widehat{a}-\frac{\tilde{a}\left(\overline{a}^2-\alpha\widehat{a}^2+(1-\alpha)\tilde{a}^2\right)}{\rho\phi\alpha\left(\overline{a}^2-\widehat{a}^2\right)}}{1+\frac{\alpha\widehat{a}+\phi\rho\tilde{a}}{\rho^2\phi^2\widehat{a}}} \tag{28}$$

If the numerator is positive, i.e., if the decrease effect of subsidy on $\widehat{a}$ is large, $\frac{d\widehat{a}}{d\tau}$ is negative. The share of individuals who use the child care service increases. The first term in the numerator shows the taxation effect. Taxation reduces demand for child care services; $\widehat{a}$ increases. The second term represents the subsidy effect. The subsidy raises the demand for child care services and $\widehat{a}$ decreases. If the subsidy effect is greater than the taxation effect, one can obtain $\frac{d\widehat{a}}{d\tau}<0$. From (27), the labor share of the child care services market increases.

In the case of subsidy, the average fertility (16) is modified to the following form:

$$n^{\alpha}=\int_{\widehat{a}}^{a}\frac{\alpha(1-\tau)aw_t}{(1-\varepsilon)z_t}\frac{1}{\overline{a}}da+\int_0^{\widehat{a}}\frac{\alpha}{\phi}\frac{1}{\overline{a}}da=\frac{\alpha\widehat{a}+\phi\rho\tilde{a}}{\phi\overline{a}} \tag{29}$$

Here, $\frac{dn^a}{d\tau}$ can be presented as shown below:

$$\frac{dn^a}{d\tau}=-\frac{\rho\tilde{a}}{\overline{a}\widehat{a}}\frac{d\widehat{a}}{d\tau} \tag{30}$$

With $\frac{d\widehat{a}}{d\tau}<0$, average fertility increases. Then, the following proposition can be established.

Proposition 3 *A subsidy for child care services can raise the share of individuals who use child care services. If $\widehat{a}$ decreases because of an increase in the share of individuals using child care services, then the average fertility can increase.*

The subsidy facilitates the use of child care services. An increase in α has a direct positive effect on fertility. However, the subsidy reduces $\widehat{a}$, which differs from the result of an increase in α by which $\widehat{a}$ rises. A decrease in $\widehat{a}$ shows an increase in $\tilde{a}$.

An increase in $\tilde{a}$ shows the share of working in the child care service sector. The wage rate of the child care sector increases, as shown by (9).

5 Discussion

Proposition 2 demonstrates that a decrease in the preference for having children, i.e., an increase in the preference for consumption in old age, does not necessarily enhance the growth rate of per capita income. This conclusion is intriguing compared to previous studies. Firstly, a decrease in the preference for having children leads to a decline in birth rates, which in turn increases per capita capital stock, mirroring the results explained in the Solow model. Furthermore, in this chapter, a decrease in the preference for having children implies an increase in the preference for consumption in old age, which produces the same effect as an increase in the survival probability considered in models accounting for survival probabilities in old age. As a result, savings for old age consumption increase, leading to capital accumulation and subsequently increasing per capita income. This finding aligns with the results of van Groezen and Meijdam (2008). However, this chapter demonstrates that when considering the endogenization of child care service prices, a decrease in the preference for having children does not necessarily lead to a decline in birth rates. In such cases, even if savings for old age consumption increase, the possibility that per capita income rises is illustrated. Theoretically, it has been shown that an increase in the population aging rate (survival probability or preference for consumption in old period) leads to an increase in per capita income, but this chapter reveals the possibility of an inverse outcome.

6 Conclusions

Our chapter presents an examination of how the preference for children affects fertility and income growth. Because of endogenous child care service pricing, an increase in preference for children cannot always raise the fertility caused by an increase in the price of child care service. This result demonstrates that even if the preference for children decreases, fertility does not always decrease. Further, that an increase in life expectancy invariably reduces fertility cannot be derived from the related literature. Therefore, income growth cannot always decrease by an increase in the preference for children because fertility cannot always increase. The dilutive effect on the capital stock does not occur.

Moreover, the subsidy for child care services increases the share of people using such services. By virtue of the subsidy policy, the fertility increases. The share of using the child care service sector increases. This result brings about an increase in the labor force participation rate.

References

Apps, P., and Rees, R. (2004). Fertility, taxation and family policy. *Scandinavian Journal of Economics, 106*(4), 745–63.

Fanti, L., and Gori, L. (2009). Population and neoclassical economic growth: A new child policy perspective. *Economics Letters, 104*(1), 27–30.

Ferrero, M. D., and Iza, M. (2004). Skill premium effects on fertility and female labor force supply. *Journal of Population Economics, 17*(1), 1–16.

Galor, O., and Weil, D. N. (1996). The gender gap, fertility, and growth. *American Economic Review, 86*(3), 374–87.

Grossman, G. M., and Yanagawa, N. (1993). Asset bubbles and endogenous growth. *Journal of Monetary Economics, 31*(1), 3–19.

Meckl, J., and Zink, S. (2004). Solow and heterogeneous labour: A neoclassical explanation of wage inequality. *Economic Journal, 114*(498), 825–43.

Romer, P. M. (1986). Increasing returns and long-run growth. *Journal of Political Economy, 94*(5), 1002–37.

Sleebos, J. (2003). *Low fertility rates in OECD countries: Facts and policy responses*. OECD Labour Market and Social Policy Occasional Papers 15, OECD Publishing.

Van Groezen, B., Leers, T., and Meijdam, L. (2003). Social security and endogenous fertility: Pensions and child allowances as Siamese twins. *Journal of Public Economics, 87*(2), 233–51.

Van Groezen, B., and Meijdam, L. (2008). Growing old and staying young: Population policy in an ageing closed economy. *Journal of Population Economics, 21*(3), 573–88.

Yakita, A. (2001). Uncertain lifetime, fertility and social security. *Journal of Population Economics, 14*(4), 635–40.

Yasuoka, M. (2020). Subsidies for elderly care with pay-as-you-go pension. *Journal of the Economics of Ageing, 17*(C).

Yasuoka, M., and Miyake, A. (2010). Change in the transition of the fertility rate. *Economics Letters, 106*, 78–80.

Masaya Shintani is an associate professor at the Faculty of Economics, Hiroshima University of Economics, specializing in social security systems and social learning theory. His research has been featured in journals including *Italian Economic Journal* and *Economics Bulletin.* He holds a Ph.D. in economics from Kobe University and earned his B.A. in economics from Hiroshima University.

Masaya Yasuoka is a professor at the School of Economics, Kwansei Gakuin University. His main areas of research interest are public finance, social security, and macroeconomics. He has published papers in scholarly journals including *Economics Letters, Economic Modelling, International Review of Economics* and *Journal of the Economics of Ageing*. Professor Yasuoka received a B.A. in economics from Nagoya City University and a Ph.D. in economics from Kobe University.

Chapter 6
Intergenerational Conflict in a Model of Endogenous Fertility

Masaya Yasuoka

1 Introduction

The fertility rate in Japan in 2021 was 1.3. Recent statistical data related to the fertility rate show a constant level, as portrayed by Fig. 1.

As presented in Fig. 1, fertility does not always show a decreasing trend in all developed countries. In some countries, the decreasing trend has stopped and fertility has increased, as in Germany. We find that the government of Germany allocates a significant portion of its expenditure to family-related policies, as shown in Fig. 2, which presents the share of Family benefits public spending to GDP.

Germany, where fertility has increased, has high expenditures related to family policies. Similarly, Sweden, where fertility has remained constant in recent years, also has high expenditures related to family policies. However, Italy and Japan, where fertility has not increased, have low expenditures related to family policies. Therefore, it can be inferred that fertility in these countries could be raised by increasing family-policy-related expenditures. However, in Japan, the size of the older population has increased and greater expenditures are needed for social security for older people.[1] Therefore, we think that a source of the revenue shortage can be addressed through child care policies for younger people.

[1] In Japan, the of ratio older people (people older than 65) to the total population is about 30%. Data: Ministry of Internal Affairs and Communications (2023).

Research for this paper was supported financially by a Grant-in-Aid for Scientific Research (No. 19530152, No. 19530237) and the University of Kitakyushu. The author is thankful to Kenji Azetsu, Takeshi Koba, Shigeki Kunieda, Kazutoshi Miyazawa, Kazunobu Muro, Tamotsu Nakamura, Takashi Oshio, Tomoya Sakagami, Jumpei Tanaka, and the seminar participants at the meeting of Japan Institute of Public Finance held at Kyoto University. Nevertheless, any remaining errors are the author's responsibility.

M. Yasuoka (✉)
School of Economics, Kwansei Gakuin University, Nishinomiya, Japan
e-mail: yasuoka@kwansei.ac.jp

M. Jinno and M. Yasuoka (eds.), *Fertility, Education and Macroeconomics: The Case of Japan*, https://doi.org/10.1007/978-981-95-1024-5_6

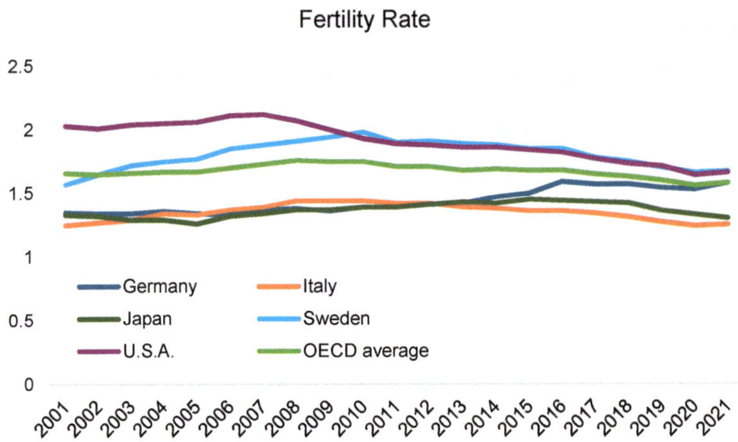

Fig. 1 Fertility rate (data: OECD Data, 2024b)

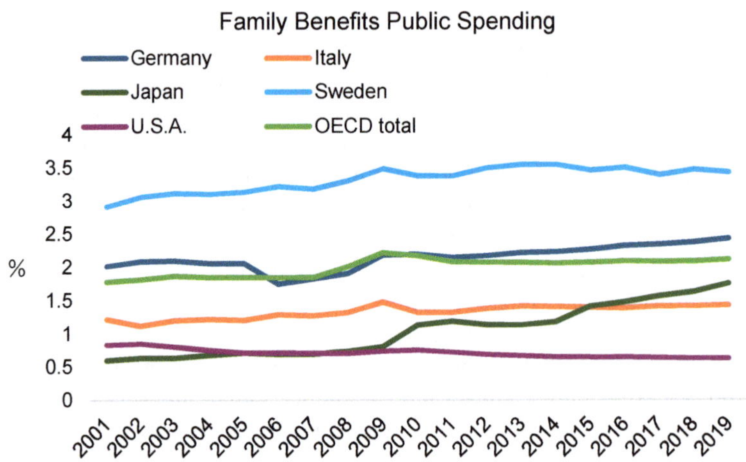

Fig. 2 Family benefits public spending (Data: OECD Data, 2024a)

Expenditures related to social security are taken from the general account. Notably, the burden on the National Treasury for social expenditures for elderly people is larger than that for social expenditures for younger people, as depicted in Fig. 3.

As shown in Fig. 3, the large elderly population in Japan results in significantly higher benefits for the elderly compared to those for the working-age population. Considering the financial burden, it is challenging to substantially increase benefits for the working-age population. However, in recent years, Japan has implemented policies such as free kindergarten and daycare. Additionally, there has been an increase in child allowances. As indicated in Fig. 2, expenditures on policies for child-rearing have been increasing in recent years.

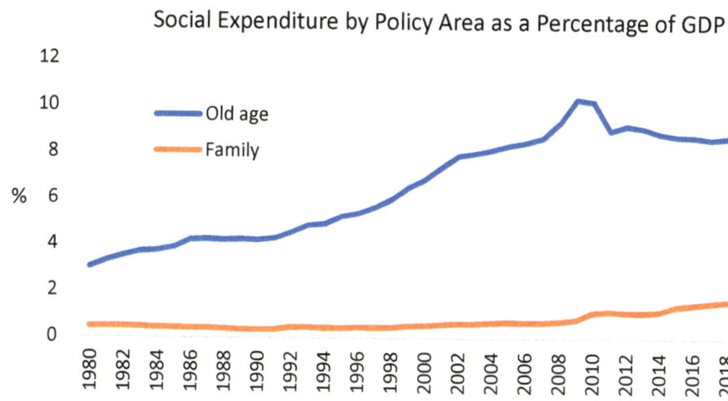

Fig. 3 Social expenditure by policy area as a percentage of GDP in Japan (Data: National Institute of Population and Social Security Research, 2021)

The level of benefits is believed to have a significant impact on birth rates. Now, how are benefits determined for the elderly and the working-age population? We can explore this through political economic analysis. Therefore, this chapter considers two models: one for the economy in which the policy variables (income tax rate and the child allowance for a child) are exogenous and the other for the economy in which the policy variables are determined according to the majority voting system. The former economy has a unique steady state in which fertility converges to or diverges from the steady state with fluctuation. The latter economy has two steady states: one for a steady state with low fertility, with policies preferred by older people, and the other for a steady state with high fertility with policies preferred by young people. The results are intuitive. If the younger population increases, this would lead to an increase in child allowances through political economic equilibrium, resulting in achieving a high fertility rate steady state. Conversely, if the older population increases, this would lead to a decrease in child allowances, resulting in achieving a low fertility rate steady state.

Some works have described how fertility affects pay-as-you-go pension systems. Van Groezen et al. (2003) and Hirazawa and Yakita (2009) describe that fertility in a decentralized economy does not coincide with that of the command optimum because of an externality brought about by the pay-as-you-go pension system under a small open economy. Van Groezen et al. (2003) show that the child allowance can improve social welfare. Oshio (2001) insists that the child allowance should be given to modify market failure under a closed economy. Yasuoka (2006) analyzes how the child allowance is financed and shows that it is not desirable to finance by the labor income taxation because the saving decreases and the capital accumulation is small. Hirazawa and Yakita (2009) report that the fertility might fluctuate and that the level of the tax rate determines whether the steady state is stable or not. On the other hand, the results presented in this chapter show that not only the level of the tax rate but also that of the child allowance determines the stability.

Bräuninger (2005), Corneo and Marquardt (2000) and Ono (2007) consider two social security systems—unemployment insurance and pensions—and analyze how these systems affect unemployment. Bräuninger (2005) shows that these two social security systems impart negative effects on the economic growth rate. Corneo and Marquardt (2000) show that if the government raises the contribution rate of the pension, high employment can be achieved, which contributes to stabilizing the economy.

Moreover, some works describe how the policy is determined politico-economically. Galasso and Profeta (2002) survey the politico-economic approach in a social security system. Konishi (2006) shows how the income tax rate and consumption tax rate are determined by the voting system when the pension is financed by the income tax and consumption tax. Hirazawa et al. (2010) show that the contribution rate of the pension rises with population aging and that the high contribution rate encourages the parents to have children under the model incorporating endogenous fertility.

This chapter is structured as follows: Sect. 2 explains the model economy, and Sect. 3 shows how the derivation of the equilibrium under the policy variables is exogenous. Section 4 presents derivation of the equilibrium under the politico-economy. Section 5 discusses the results obtained by this chapter and the situation in Japan. The final section concludes this chapter.

2 Model

Three agents exist in this economy: households, firms, and a government. This model economy consists of a two-period (young and old) overlapping generations model.

2.1 Households

We assume representative households. Each exists for two periods: young and old. Younger people in t period gain utility from young consumption c_{1t}, old consumption c_{2t+1}, and the number of children n_t. We assume the utility function as

$$u_t = \alpha \ln c_{1t} + \beta \ln n_t + \gamma \ln c_{2t+1}, \quad 0 < \alpha, \beta, \gamma < 1. \tag{1}$$

where β and γ respectively denote the utility weight of having children and the discount rate. This utility function form is assumed in Eckstein and Wolpin (1985), Galor and Weil (1996), van Groezen et al. (2003), and others.

We assume that child care time is needed for a child care of ϕ unit time to have a child and child care goods z.[2] This chapter assumes that each household supplies a unit of labor. However, child care time reduces the labor supply, as Galor and Weil (1996) and Ferrero and Iza (2004) report. The labor time presents $1 - \phi n_t$ when the household has n_t children. The government imposes labor income taxation at the τ rate. The revenue is allocated for the child allowance and income transfer for older people. Also, q denotes the child allowance for a child; p_t represents the income transfer for older people. Moreover, the government runs a pay-as-you-go pension system and collects a fee p from younger people. Denoting N_{t+1} as the younger population size in $t + 1$ period and N_t as the older population size, the pension benefit of old people is $\frac{N_{t+1}}{N_t}$. Defining $\overline{n}_t$ as average fertility, we obtain $\frac{N_{t+1}}{N_t} = \overline{n}_t$. Then, the household budget constraint is shown as

$$(z - q)n_t + c_{1t} + \frac{c_{2t+1}}{1 + r_{t+1}} = (1 - \phi n_t)(1 - \tau)w_t - p + \frac{\overline{n}_t p + p_{t+1}}{1 + r_{t+1}} \tag{2}$$

where r_{t+1} is an interest rate. Households supply labor. In addition, w_t denotes the wage rate. Households decide the allocation of c_{1t}, c_{2t+1}, n_t to maximize their utility subject to budget constraint and are given an average fertility which is a pension earning rate.[3] The derived allocations are

$$c_{1t} = \frac{\alpha}{\alpha + \beta + \gamma}\left((1 - \tau)w_t - p + \frac{\overline{n}_t p + p_{t+1}}{1 + r_{t+1}}\right) \tag{3}$$

$$c_{2t+1} = \frac{\gamma(1 + r_{t+1})}{\alpha + \beta + \gamma}\left((1 - \tau)w_t - p + \frac{\overline{n}_t p + p_{t+1}}{1 + r_{t+1}}\right) \tag{4}$$

$$n_t = \frac{\frac{\beta}{\alpha+\beta+\gamma}\left((1 - \tau)w_t - p + \frac{\overline{n}_t p + p_{t+1}}{1+r_{t+1}}\right)}{z - q + \phi(1 - \tau)w_t} \tag{5}$$

Considering a symmetric household, we obtain $n_t = \overline{n}_t$.. Therefore, the number of children (fertility) is represented as

$$n_t = \frac{\frac{\beta}{\alpha+\beta+\gamma}\left((1 - \tau)w_t - p + \frac{p_{t+1}}{1+r_{t+1}}\right)}{z - q + \phi(1 - \tau)w_t - \frac{\beta}{\alpha+\beta+\gamma}\frac{p}{1+r_{t+1}}} \tag{6}$$

This economy incorporates market failure because of the pay-as-you-go pension system. Not considering that each household's children affect the earning rate of pension system, each household chooses the number of children n_t. We omit the

---

[2] Van Groezen et al. (2003) assume that only child care goods are necessary to have children. However, Galor and Weil (1996) assume only child care time as a necessity to have children.

[3] As Oshio (2001) and van Groezen, Leers and Meijdam (2003) detail, household's optimal allocations are derived under a given average fertility rate, which is an earning rate of pension.

proof showing that the allocations in a decentralized economy do not coincide with those of the command optimum because Oshio (2001) and van Groezen et al. (2003) have already described them. Oshio (2001) and van Groezen et al. (2003) insist upon giving the child allowance to parents to modify market failure.

2.2 Firms

Final goods Y_t are produced by inputting capital stock K_t and labor L_t. The production function is assumed as

$$Y_t = AK_t^{\theta}L_t^{1-\theta},\ 0 < A,\ 0 < \theta < 1. \tag{7}$$

Considering the fertility n_t, labor input is $L_t = (1 - \phi n_t)N_t$. With perfect competition, the wage rate w_t and the interest rate r_t are

$$w_t = (1 - \theta)k_t^{\theta}, \tag{8}$$

$$1 + r_t = \theta k_t^{\theta-1} \tag{9}$$

where $k_t = \frac{K_t}{L_t}$, and capital stock depreciates fully in one period.

2.3 Government

The government not only runs a pay-as-you-go pension system; it also collects a labor income tax to give a child allowance for childcare support or to give income to the older generation. Assuming the balanced budget constraint, the government budget constraint is

$$N_t\tau(1 - \phi n_t)w_t = N_tqn_t + N_{t-1}p_t \rightarrow p_{t+1} = n_t(\tau w_t - (\tau\phi w_t + q)n_{t+1}) \tag{10}$$

If the child allowance for a child q or younger generation's fertility n_{t+1} is large given a certain tax revenue, then the income transfer for the older generation is small either because the share of the child allowance to total government expenditure is large or a short labor time decreases tax revenue. We therefore find an intergenerational conflict that occurs between younger people and older people. A large child allowance is desired by younger people, but older people want to receive as large an income transfer as possible.

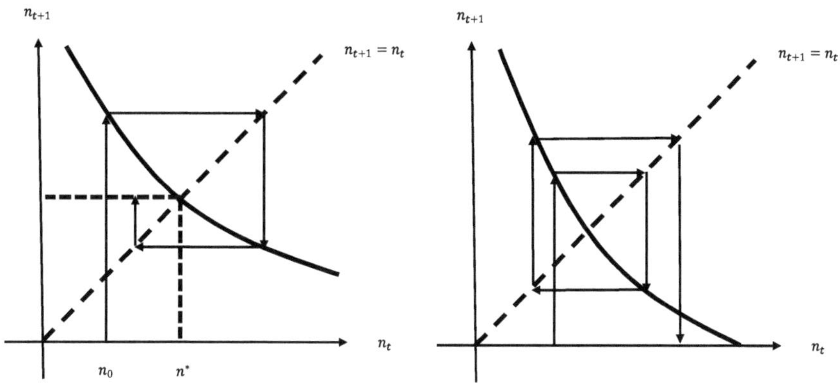

Fig. 4 (1) Dynamics of n_t (a stable case). (2) Dynamics of n_t (an unstable case)

3 Equilibrium

These analyses assume a small open economy, i.e., the interest rate and wage rate are given as exogenous. Therefore, the equilibrium in this economy is given by fertility dynamics with (6) and (10).

$$n_{t+1} = \frac{1+r}{\tau\phi w + q} \left(\left(\frac{(1-\tau)w - p}{n_t} + \frac{p + \tau w}{1+r} \right) - \frac{(\alpha+\beta+\gamma)(z - q + \phi(1-\tau)w)}{\beta} \right) \quad (11)$$

The dynamics of n_t is depicted as Fig. 4.

We find that the fertility fluctuates over time. If $\frac{dn_{t+1}}{dn_t} > -1$, that is, $\frac{1+r}{\tau\phi w+q} \frac{(1-\tau)w-p}{(n^*)^2} < 1$, then the dynamics of n_t converges to a steady state (Fig. 4-1), where n^* denotes the fertility at the steady state.[4] However, the stable condition does not hold, and the dynamics of n_t diverge from the steady state with fluctuation (Fig. 4-2). If the child allowance q is large and the fertility at the steady state n^* is large, this condition holds. If the child allowance q becomes large, then the dynamics of the fertility n_t change from divergence with fluctuation to convergence with fluctuation. However, an increase in the child allowance does not always pull up the steady state fertility for the following reasons. The large child allowance q makes the income transfer for older people small. Fertility decreases if the income becomes small. Therefore, if this negative effect is large, an increase in the child allowance q reduces the steady state fertility. As described above, we obtain the following proposition.

[4] We show the condition of $\frac{p+\tau w}{1+r} - \frac{\alpha+\beta+\gamma}{\beta}(z - q + \phi(1-\tau)w)$ as the stable condition. See Appendix A for a detailed proof.

Proposition 1 If the government collects tax revenue to provide a child allowance for younger people and an income transfer for older people, the fertility converges to or diverges from the steady state with fluctuation.

Fertility fluctuates for the following reasons. If the child care time is fixed and tax revenue is used only for income transfer for older people, fertility does not fluctuate, and fertility is constant over time. However, if the child care time varies according to the number of children and the child allowance is given for younger people, then fertility fluctuates. The current fertility is determined by future fertility. Households consider the lifetime income and decide to have a number of children, but the lifetime income contains income transfer for older people in the future from the government. If there are many children in the future generation, then fertility becomes low because the lifetime income becomes small as a result of the small income transfer for older people because the decrease in labor time decreases the tax revenue and increases the ratio of the child allowance. Therefore, if the fertility in period $t+1$ is high, then the fertility in t period is low.

On the other hand, if the fertility in $t+1$ period is low, then the fertility in t period is high because if the future fertility is low, the labor time is high, so the tax revenue is also large. Therefore, the income transfer for older people is also large and the current fertility is high because of the high lifetime income.

Hirazawa and Yakita (2009) show that the fertility dynamics might fluctuate, as this chapter also shows, under the model economy that all tax revenue is used for the income transfer to older people. The result in this chapter that the income transfer for older people makes the fertility fluctuate is the same as that of Hirazawa and Yakita (2009). However, we consider the child allowance and show that the child allowance determines the local stability of the steady state.

This section suggests the above results under a fixed tax rate and the child allowance for a child. However, the next section derives how the dynamics of fertility is determined if the policy variables (the child allowance and income transfer) are determined by the majority voting system reflecting each generation's preferences.

4 Equilibrium Under a Majority Voting System

This section presents derivation of the equilibrium under the majority voting system. In this economy, two types of groups exist: a younger generation and an older generation; the policy which the majority group favors is adopted. First, we consider the policy favored by the younger generation. Voters of the younger generation favor not income transfer for older people but child allowance. The indirect utility function of the younger generation v_t can therefore be represented as follows:

$$v_t = const. + (\alpha + \gamma)\ln\left(\frac{(1-\tau_t)w - p + \frac{p_{t+1}}{1+r}}{n_t} + \frac{p}{1+r}\right) + (\alpha + \beta + \gamma)\ln n_t$$

where

$$const. = \alpha\ln\alpha + \gamma\ln\gamma - (\alpha+\gamma)\ln(\alpha+\beta+\gamma) + \gamma\ln(1+r),$$

$$n_t = \frac{\frac{\beta}{\alpha+\beta+\gamma}\left((1-\tau)w - p + \frac{p_{t+1}}{1+r}\right) + \tau_t w}{z + \phi w - \frac{\beta}{\alpha+\beta+\gamma}\frac{p}{1+r}}.$$

Therein, p_{t+1} denotes the income transfer when younger people become old. Younger people select the tax rate to maximize their utility τ subject to given p_{t+1}. They select the tax rate τ under no income transfer for older people in this period, that is the government budget constraint $\tau_t(1-\phi n_t)w = qn_t$ because the expenditure for older people is by no means a source of satisfaction for younger people (it does not increase their utility).

The tax rate is determined to hold $\frac{\partial v_t}{\partial \tau_t} = 0$.[5]

$$n_t\left(z + \phi w - \frac{\alpha+2\beta+\gamma}{\alpha+\beta+\gamma}\frac{p}{1+r}\right) = \frac{\beta}{\alpha+\beta+\gamma}\left((1-\tau_t)w - p + \frac{p_{t+1}}{1+r}\right)$$

Considering a certain parameter, the tax rate selected by younger people is in $0 < \tau_t < 1$.

Second, we derive the tax rate selected by older people. They have no interest in the child allowance and favor as large an income transfer as possible. Income transfer is $p_t = \tau n_{t-1}(1-\phi n_t)w$. They select the tax rate to maximize the income transfer per older person p_t subject to given n_{t-1} to hold the following equation[6]:

$$\frac{z + \phi(1-\tau_t)w - \frac{\beta}{\alpha+\beta+\gamma}\frac{p}{1+r}}{\phi\tau_t w} = \frac{-\frac{\beta}{\alpha+\beta+\gamma} + \phi n_t}{1-\phi n_t}$$

If $\frac{\partial n_t}{\partial \tau_t} > 0$, then the tax rate which holds the above condition is in $0 < \tau_t < 1$. Furthermore, τ_t is shown as the function of n_t.

We derive the policies selected respectively by younger and older people. However, the relative population size of each generation decides which policies are carried out. If $\frac{N_t}{N_{t-1}} < 1$, that is $n_{t-1} < 1$, then the population size of older people is larger than that of younger people, so the policy favored by older people is conducted. On the other hand, if $n_{t-1} > 1$, then the population size of younger people is larger than that of older people, so the policy favored by younger people is conducted. We consider the plane of n_t and n_{t+1}; that is, n_{t-1} and n_t changes to n_t and n_{t+1}, respectively. Based on $n_t = 1$, the dynamics of fertility differ, as shown

[5] See Appendix B for a detailed proof.

[6] See Appendix C for a detailed proof.

below[7]:

$$n_{t+1} = \frac{\frac{\beta}{\alpha+\beta+\gamma}((1-\tau(n_{t+1}))w - p) + \tau(n_{t+1})w}{z + \phi w - \frac{\beta}{\alpha+\beta+\gamma}\frac{p}{1+r}} \quad \textit{if } n_t \geq 1. \tag{12}$$

$$\begin{aligned} n_{t+1} = &\frac{1+r}{\tau(n_t)\phi w}\left(\frac{(1-\tau(n_{t+1}))w - p}{n_t} + \frac{p + \tau(n_t)w}{1+r}\right) \\ &- \frac{1+r}{\tau(n_t)\phi w}\frac{\alpha+\beta+\gamma}{\beta}(z + \phi(1-\tau(n_t))w) \quad \textit{if } n_t < 1. \end{aligned} \tag{13}$$

Figure 5-1 shows the case for which the model economy has two steady state equilibria under the given initial fertility of n_0.[8] Figure 5-1 shows that two steady state equilibria exist: one for the steady state with high fertility and the other for the steady state with low fertility. The steady state with low fertility is not always stable. If the equilibrium is stable and the initial fertility is given by $n_0 < 1$, then the fertility dynamics converge to the steady state with low fertility. On the other hand, if the initial fertility is $n_0 < 1$ and the steady state with n^{low} is not stable, then the fertility dynamics converge to the steady state with high fertility (Fig. 5-2). Consequently, we obtain the following proposition.

Proposition 2 The economy with a majority voting system brings about two steady state equilibria: one steady state has a high fertility, conducting a policy favored by younger people; the other has a steady state with low fertility, conducting a policy favored by older people.

We can understand this proposition intuitively. Younger people favor the child allowance policy: it raises fertility. Therefore, fertility is high as long as a policy favored by younger people is conducted. On the other hand, older people favor income transfer policy. In this case, no child allowance exists. Consequently, fertility is low.[9]

The description above explains only the case in which there are two steady state equilibria; however, the model economy does not always have two steady states in reality. For example, without the steady state with high fertility, the fertility dynamics converge to the steady state with low fertility if this state is stable (Fig. 5-3). On the other hand, for the case of no steady state with low fertility, even if initial fertility is

[7] Originally, (13) is shown by $n_{t+1} = \frac{1+r}{\tau(n_{t+1})\phi w}\left(\frac{(1-\tau(n_t))w-p}{n_t} + \frac{p+\tau(n_t)w}{1+r}\right) - \frac{1+r}{\tau(n_{t+1})\phi w}\frac{(\alpha+\beta+\gamma)(z+\phi(1-\tau(n_t))w)}{\beta}$. However, $\tau(n_{t+1})$ is determined by n_{t+1}, n_{t+1} is given by n_t. We can thus consider $\tau(n_{t+1})$ as the function of n_t.

[8] The form of (13) is not always downward sloping. If $(1-\tau(n_t))$ at the start of the bracket changes greatly for the change of n_t, then the form of (13) might be upward sloping (see Appendix D for detailed proof). We assume the sufficient condition to depict the dynamics of n_t as shown in Fig. 5 in $n_t < 1$.

[9] Fertility might be raised by the increase in lifetime income because of the increase in income transfer. In this case, no steady state exists with low fertility.

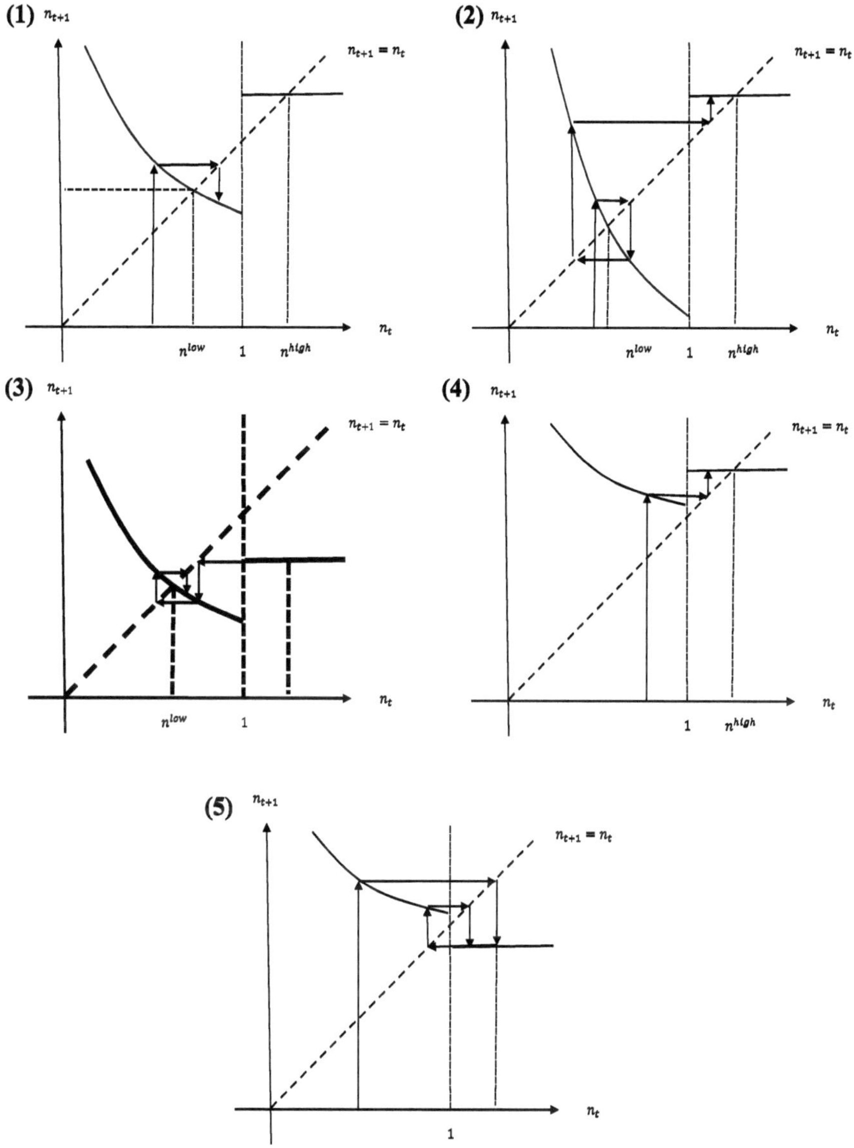

Fig. 5 (1) Dynamics n_t under a majority voting system (two stable steady state equilibria). (2) Dynamics n_t under a majority voting system (stable and unstable steady state equilibria). (3) Dynamics n_t under a majority voting system (only n^{low} steady state equilibrium). (4) Dynamics n_t under a majority voting system (only n^{high} steady state equilibrium). (5) Dynamics n_t under a majority voting system (no steady state equilibrium)

low, fertility dynamics might converge to the steady state with high fertility (Fig. 5-4). If there is no steady state with either low fertility or high fertility, the fertility dynamics n_t will cycle in the long run (Fig. 5-5).

5 Discussion

In Japan, where the elderly population is significantly large, it is realistic to consider the initial population ratio $n_0 < 1$. In this scenario, as shown in Fig. 5-1, the system converges to a steady state with a low fertility. Japan continues to experience this low fertility, and it can be said that the results brought about by both reality and the theoretical model are consistent. Furthermore, as indicated in Fig. 2, the benefits for the elderly generation are greater than those for the younger generation, which can also be explained as a political-economic equilibrium.

On the other hand, in recent years, Japan has been considering measures such as the free provision of nursery and kindergarten education and the increase of child allowances. While these policies might seem partially inconsistent with the model in this chapter, which accounts for advancing aging, it remains a fact that there is a significant difference in the level of benefits between the elderly and younger generations. This substantial difference can be said to be a result of the political-economic equilibrium presented in this chapter.

It is worth noting that there is also a probabilistic voting model, which determines policy variables to maximize social welfare by weighting the population of each generation. In such a model, the conclusion where benefits to the younger generation are zero when the elderly population is large, and vice versa, does not arise. Instead, benefits to the younger generation can be achieved as a political-economic equilibrium even when the elderly population is large. Analyzing using a probabilistic voting model can also be considered a valid approach.

6 Conclusions

This chapter described an overlapping generations model introducing endogenous fertility. It also presented that fewer children in a society engenders fewer children in an economy with two equilibria: one for the economy in which the policy variables are exogenous and the other for the economy in which the policy is determined by the majority voting system. We analyzed how fertility changes and how the policy including income transfers for older people and childcare support affects younger and older population ratios in each model.

Results of these analyses suggest the following conclusions. The intergenerational population ratio changes endogenously in the endogenous fertility model. The model economy with policy variables that are exogenous—the income tax rate and the child allowance—has a unique steady state. Therefore, the fertility converges to or diverges from the steady state with fluctuation. The level of the income tax rate and the child allowance determine whether the steady state is stable or not. However, considered politico-economically, if the population size of older people constitutes a majority, the bulk of tax revenues are allocated to income transfer for this group because the government must carry out a policy favored by older people as a result of the highly influential voice of this group. A greater child allowance is awarded to parents if younger people are the majority.

In Japan, fertility is at a low level, with insufficient child allowances pointed out as one reason for this. The population ratio of older people is also increasing, and this group prefers policies brought about for its benefit. This chapter demonstrates this fact using analyses of a model economy.

Appendix

Appendix A: Stable Condition

Considering a steady state, we can show (11) as follows:

$$1 = \frac{1+r}{\tau\phi w + q}\frac{(1-\tau)w - p}{(n^*)^2} + \frac{1+r}{\tau\phi w + q}\left(\frac{p+\tau w}{1+r} - \frac{(\alpha+\beta+\gamma)(z-q+\phi(1-\tau)w)}{\beta}\right)\frac{1}{n^*} \quad (14)$$

Considering (14), the stable condition $\frac{1+r}{\tau\phi w+q}\frac{(1-\tau)w-p}{(n^*)^2}$ is written as

$$\frac{p+\tau w}{1+r} - \frac{(\alpha+\beta+\gamma)(z-q+\phi(1-\tau)w)}{\beta} > 0 \quad (15)$$

Appendix B: Derivation of the Tax Rate to Maximize the Utility of Younger People

We derive $\frac{\partial v_t}{\partial \tau_t}$ as follows:

$$\frac{\partial v_t}{\partial \tau_t} = -(\alpha+\gamma)\frac{\frac{w}{n_t} + \left((1-\tau_t)w - p + \frac{p_{t+1}}{1+r}\right)\frac{\partial n_t}{\partial \tau_t}\frac{1}{n_t^2}}{\frac{(1-\tau_t)w-p+\frac{p_{t+1}}{1+r}}{n_t} + \frac{p}{1+r}} + (\alpha+\beta+\gamma)\frac{\frac{\partial n_t}{\partial \tau_t}}{n_t} = 0. \quad (16)$$

where $\frac{\partial n_t}{\partial \tau_t} = \frac{\frac{\alpha+\gamma}{\alpha+\beta+\gamma}w}{z+\phi w-\frac{\beta}{\alpha+\beta+\gamma}\frac{p}{1+r}}$. The tax rate to maximize the utility of younger people is derived as $\frac{\partial v_t}{\partial \tau_t}$ as

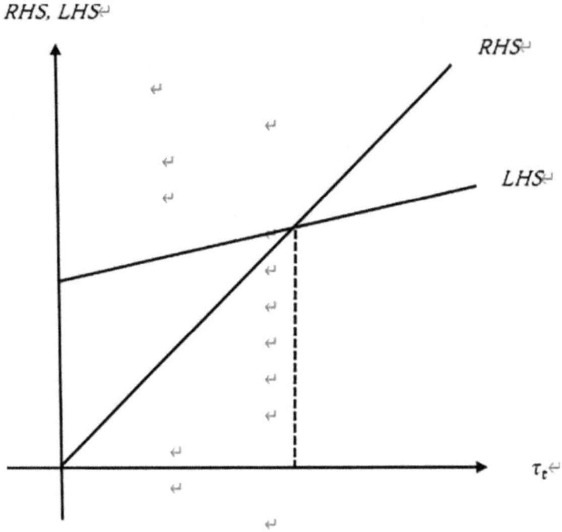

Fig. 6 Tax rate τ_t, selected by younger people

$$\left(z + \phi w - \frac{\alpha + 2\beta + \gamma}{\alpha + \beta + \gamma}\frac{p}{1 + r}\right)n_t = \frac{\beta}{\alpha + \beta + \gamma}\left((1 - \tau_t)w - p + \frac{p_{t+1}}{1 + r}\right). \quad (17)$$

or

$$\frac{\frac{\beta}{\alpha+\beta+\gamma}\left((1 - \tau_t)w - p + \frac{p_{t+1}}{1+r}\right) + \tau_t w}{z + \phi w - \frac{\beta}{\alpha+\beta+\gamma}\frac{p}{1+r}} = \frac{(1 + r)\tau_t w}{p} \quad (18)$$

As shown in Fig. 6, the tax rate τ_t exists under certain parameters, i.e., $\frac{1+r}{p} > \frac{\alpha+\gamma}{\alpha+\beta+\gamma}$.

We consider p_{t+1} as given. We obtain $p_{t+1} = 0$ if the $n_t > 1$ for any periods. Then, the straight line of n_t which holds $n_t > 1$ in Fig. 5, can be depicted.

Appendix C: Derivation of the Tax Rate Selected by Older People

Older people prefer the tax rate τ_t to maximize the income transfer $p_t = n_{t-1}(1 - \phi n_t)\tau_t w$. We obtain the condition given by $\frac{dv_t}{d\tau_t} = 0$ as

$$\frac{z + \phi(1 - \tau_t)w - \frac{\beta}{\alpha+\beta+\gamma}\frac{p}{1+r}}{\phi\tau_t w} = \frac{-\frac{\beta}{\alpha+\beta+\gamma} + \phi n_t}{1 - \phi n_t} \quad (19)$$

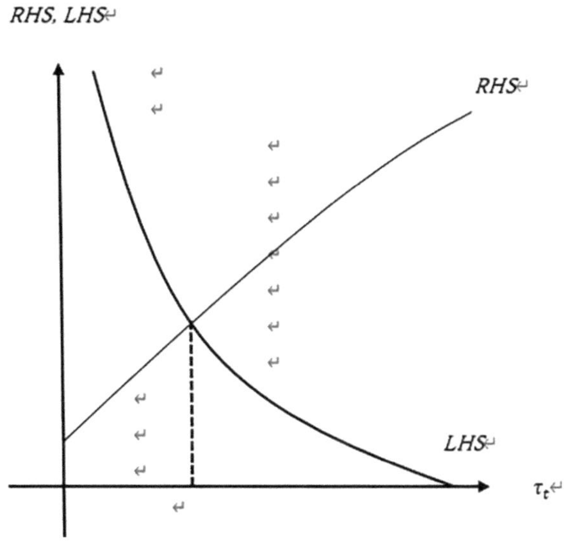

Fig. 7 Tax rate τ_t, selected by older people

We assume the condition $\frac{dn_t}{d\tau_t} > 0$ for existence of the tax rate τ_t in $0 < \tau_t < 1$. Without this condition, the tax rate selected by older people is $\tau_t = 1$, which is impractical. Actually, $\frac{dn_t}{d\tau_t}$ is shown as

$$\frac{dn_t}{d\tau_t} = \frac{\frac{\beta w}{\alpha+\beta+\gamma}\left(-z + \frac{\beta}{\alpha+\beta+\gamma}\frac{p}{1+r} - \phi p + \frac{\phi p_{t+1}}{1+r}\right)}{\left(z + \phi(1-\tau_t)w - \frac{\beta}{\alpha+\beta+\gamma}\frac{p}{1+r}\right)^2}. \tag{20}$$

If $-z + \frac{\beta}{\alpha+\beta+\gamma}\frac{p}{1+r} - \phi p + \frac{\phi p_{t+1}}{1+r} > 0$ holds, then $\frac{dn_t}{d\tau_t} > 0$. Assuming this condition, the tax rate τ_t is depicted in Fig. 7.

Appendix D: Dynamics of n_t in $n_t < 1$

We obtain $\frac{dn_{t+1}}{dn_t}$ as follows:

$$\begin{aligned}\frac{dn_{t+1}}{dn_t} &= -\frac{n_{t+1}}{\tau_t}\frac{\partial \tau_t}{\partial n_t} \\ &\quad - \frac{1+r}{\tau_t \phi w}\left(\frac{n_t w \frac{\partial \tau_t}{\partial n_t} + ((1-\tau_t)w - p)}{n_t^2} - \frac{\partial \tau_t}{\partial n_t} w\left(\frac{1}{1+r} + \frac{\phi(\alpha+\beta+\gamma)}{\beta}\right)\right)\end{aligned} \tag{21}$$

If the absolute value of $w\frac{\partial\tau_t}{dn_t}\left(\frac{1}{1+r}+\frac{\phi(\alpha+\beta+\gamma)}{\beta}\right)$ is considerably large, the sign of $\frac{dn_{t+1}}{dn_t}$ might be positive. However, we assume $\frac{dn_{t+1}}{dn_t}<0$.

Moreover, we derive $\frac{\partial^2 n_{t+1}}{dn_t^2}$.

$$\begin{aligned}\frac{\partial^2 n_{t+1}}{dn_t^2}=&-\frac{1}{\tau_t}\left(-\frac{n_{t+1}}{\tau_t}\left(\frac{\partial\tau_t}{dn_t}\right)^2+\frac{\partial\tau_t}{dn_t}\frac{dn_{t+1}}{dn_t}+\frac{\partial^2\tau_t}{dn_t^2}\right)\\&-\frac{1}{\tau_t^2}\frac{1+r}{\phi w}\frac{\partial\tau_t}{dn_t}\left(-\frac{wn_t\frac{\partial\tau_t}{dn_t}+((1-\tau_t)w-p)}{n_t}+w\frac{\partial\tau_t}{dn_t}\left(\frac{1}{1+r}+\frac{\phi(\alpha+\beta+\gamma)}{\beta}\right)\right)\\&+\frac{1+r}{\tau_t\phi w}\left(\frac{-n_t^2\frac{\partial^2\tau_t}{dn_t^2}+2\left(n_t w\frac{\partial\tau_t}{dn_t}+((1-\tau_t)w-p)\right)}{n_t^3}+w\frac{\partial^2\tau_t}{dn_t^2}\left(\frac{1}{1+r}+\frac{\phi(\alpha+\beta+\gamma)}{\beta}\right)\right)\end{aligned}\tag{22}$$

With $\frac{dn_{t+1}}{dn_t}<0$ and $\frac{\partial^2 n_{t+1}}{dn_t^2}>0$, we depict the dynamics of n_t as Fig. 5 in $n_t<1$.

References

Bräuninger, M. (2005). Social security, unemployment, and growth. *International Tax and Public Finance, 12*, 423–34.

Corneo, G., and Marquardt, M. (2000). Public pensions, unemployment insurance, and growth. *Journal of Public Economics, 75*, 293–311.

Eckstein, Z., and Wolpin, K. I. (1985). Endogenous fertility and optimal population size. *Journal of Public Economics, 27*, 93–106.

Ferrero M. D., and Iza, A. (2004). Skill premium effects on fertility and female labor force supply. *Journal of Population Economics, 17*, 1–16.

Galasso, V., and Profeta P. (2002). The political economy of social security: A survey. *European Journal of Political Economy, 18*, 1–29.

Galor, O., and Weil, D. N. (1996). The gender gap, fertility, and growth. *American Economic Review, 86*, 374–87.

Hirazawa, M., Kitaura, K., and Yakita, A. (2010). Aging, fertility, social security and political equilibrium. *Journal of Population Economics, 23*(2), 559–69.

Hirazawa, M., and Yakita, A. (2009). Fertility, child care outside the home, and pay-as-you-go social security. *Journal of Population Economics, 22*(3), 565–83.

Konishi, H. (2006). Shakaihoshou no kibo to zaigenchoutatsu, seijikeizaigakutekibunseki [Financing of the social security: A politico-economic approach]. *Kikan Shakaihoshou kenkyu* [*Quarterly of Social Security Research*], *42*(1), 4–16.

Ono, T. (2007). Unemployment dynamics in an OLG economy with public pensions. *Economic Theory, 33*, 549–77.

Oshio, T. (2001). Ikujishien・nenkinkaikaku to shusshoritsu [Child-care support, pension reform, and fertility]. *Kikan ShakaiHosho Kenkyu* [*Quarterly of Social Security Research*], *36*(4), 434–546.

Van Groezen, B., Leers, T., and Meijdam L. (2003). Social security and endogenous fertility: Pensions and child allowances as Siamese twins. *Journal of Public Economics, 87*, 233–51.

Yasuoka, M. (2006). Shusshoritsu to kazeiseisaku no kankei [The relationship between the fertility rate and tax policy]. *Kikan Shakaihoshou Kenkyu* [*Quarterly of Social Security Research*], *42*(1), 80–90.

Data

Ministry of Internal Affairs and Communications. (2023). Toukei topikkusu No. 138 Toukeikaramita wagakuni no koreisha [Statistics topics No. 138: The elderly in Japan from a statistical perspective]. https://www.stat.go.jp/data/topics/pdf/topics138.pdf
National Institute of Population and Social Security Research. (2021). Shakai hoshou hiyou toukei [Statistics on social security costs]. https://www.ipss.go.jp/ss-cost/j/fsss-R03/fsss_R03.html
OECD Data. (2024a). Family benefits public spending. https://data.oecd.org/socialexp/family-benefits-public-spending.htm
OECD Data. (2024b). Fertility rates. https://data.oecd.org/pop/fertility-rates.htm

Masaya Yasuoka is a professor at the School of Economics, Kwansei Gakuin University. His main areas of research interest are public finance, social security, and macroeconomics. He has published papers in scholarly journals including *Economics Letters*, *Economic Modelling*, *International Review of Economics* and *Journal of the Economics of Ageing*. Professor Yasuoka received a B.A. in economics from Nagoya City University and a Ph.D. in economics from Kobe University.

Chapter 7
The Effects of Admitting Immigrants on the Welfare of Each Generation of Natives: Considering the Additional Burden of Education and the Indirect Impact Through the Pension System

Masaya Yasuoka and Masatoshi Jinno

1 Introduction

This research explores the impact of immigrant admission on the welfare of native residents. It utilizes simulation methods to analyze two primary factors: the imperfect substitutability between native and immigrant workers in a Pay-As-You-Go (PAYG) pension system, and the increased strain on the education system due to immigrant children.

The traditional textbook model of immigration, where native and foreign-born workers are seen as perfectly substitutable, suggests that admitting immigrants fundamentally lowers native wage levels due to this presumed perfect substitutability in identical education and experience groups. Studies like those by Borjas (2003) and Borjas and Katz (2007), based on this idea, conclude that immigrants reduce native wages. However, this notion of perfect interchangeability between native and immigrant workers within the same skill and experience categories is quite strong. Contrarily, Ottaviano and Peri (2008, 2012) found that immigrants ultimately raise the average wages of natives, considering the imperfect substitutability between these groups. Echoing this, Powell (2015) argued that immigrant and native labor in the

This study was funded by the Ministry of Education, Culture, Sports, Science, and Technology of Japan (JSPS grant number: KAKENHI 19K01636).

M. Yasuoka
School of Economics, Kwansei Gakuin University, Nishinomiya, Japan
e-mail: yasuoka@kwansei.ac.jp

M. Jinno (✉)
Department of Economics, Nanzan University, Nagoya, Japan
e-mail: jimasato@nanzan-u.ac.jp

M. Jinno and M. Yasuoka (eds.), *Fertility, Education and Macroeconomics: The Case of Japan*, https://doi.org/10.1007/978-981-95-1024-5_7

same educational and experiential bracket are likely imperfect substitutes, in line with Ottaviano and Peri's findings, as opposed to the perfect substitutability assumed by Borjas and others. This is supported by empirical studies like Card (2009) and Dustmann, Frattini, and Preston (2013), demonstrating that immigrant language skills typically lag behind those of natives.

Furthermore, Dustmann et al. (2016) revealed the reasons behind differing outcomes in studies on immigration's impact on wages, highlighting potential misclassification issues. This occurs even with the assumption of imperfect substitutability between immigrants and natives, as immigrants are often "downgraded" in the same education category (the skill-cell approach). The study also indicates that this downgrading likely leads to an exaggerated perception of the negative wage impact on natives, particularly with the skill-cell approach. Conversely, it results in an underestimation of the overall wage impact on natives when a structural approach is used. Dustmann et al. (2016) therefore suggest focusing on the broader impact of immigration on native wages, rather than just group-specific effects. Additionally, Silas (2020) examined wage disparities between migrants and locals in 49 countries pre-COVID-19, finding an average 12.6% wage gap favoring natives in high-income nations, based on mean hourly wages. Immigrants typically enter these high-income countries at lower wage rates. Consequently, immigrants should not be seen as substitutable with natives in the same skill-cell. Instead, they should be viewed as distinct substitutable production factors, recognizing the "downgrading" factor when assessing immigration's impact on native welfare.

Consequently, this study adopts a production function model where the total labor supplies of natives and immigrants are only imperfectly substitutable. In this model, native workers' incomes are typically higher than those of immigrants. This approach aligns with the methodologies used in Guerreiro et al. (2020) and Llull (2020).[1]

In studies assessing the impact of accepting foreign workers, the emphasis has largely been on the effects on wage and unemployment rates, as seen in works like Powell (2015) and Llull (2020). Yet, an exclusive focus on wage rates proves insufficient for a comprehensive analysis of the impact on native welfare in nations with PAYG pension systems. The influence of immigration on the welfare of successive generations, affected by factors like the heightened costs of educating immigrant children and possible alterations in wage rates, remains underexplored.

It is not a given that all immigrants will eventually return to their home country or move to another; many remain and start families in their host countries, such as Japan.[2] This results in an added challenge for native residents, particularly in

[1] Guerreiro, Rebelo, and Teles (2020) examined the most beneficial immigrant policy for native welfare in an economy where the government implements an optimal redistributive welfare system and provides public goods. In their model, the degree of substitutability between natives and immigrants is crucial. This is because immigrants can both decrease and enhance native productivity through the production function—a stark contrast to scenarios of perfect substitutability. Llull (2020) utilized this production function framework to explain the varying conclusions of studies by Borjas (2003), Borjas and Katz (2007), and Ottaviano and Peri (2008, 2012).

[2] In the case of foreign workers, some may remain only for short-term labor supply, while others may form families and continue to reside long-term. Dustmann and Görlach (2016) and Jinno and

raising and educating immigrant children who may not be well-acquainted with the host country's culture and language. Consequently, educators are often required to extend extra cultural and linguistic support to these children, aiding their adaptation to life in the host country.

The Organization for Economic Cooperation and Development (OECD, 2019) disclosed that about 48% of 15-year-old first- and second-generation immigrant students in OECD countries did not speak the PISA test language at home, leading to an average reading score of 452, which is 42 points lower than their non-immigrant peers. In some countries, students who underachieve must often repeat a grade. According to the OECD (2020), 11% of 15-year-olds in these countries in 2018 had repeated a grade at least once in their compulsory education. Additionally, the OECD (2020) identified a negative link between grade repetition and developing a growth mindset.[3]

In countries like Japan, hardly any 15-year-olds reported grade repetition.[4] The OECD (2016) attributes Japan's success to its educational approach, where teachers not only identify but also provide additional support to struggling students within and beyond regular school hours. This study concentrates on the costs of the supplementary support provided by additional teachers for immigrant children to meet a minimum educational standard, detailed later in this chapter.

Zinovyeva et al. (2014), along with Bernhofer and Tonin (2022), found that immigrant children and students learning in a language different from their mother tongue generally underperform compared to natives or those educated in their native language. Analyzing PISA data from 2003, 2006, and 2009, Zinovyeva et al. (2014) observed this underperformance among immigrant children. Bernhofer and Tonin (2022) further noted that taking exams in a second language results in a roughly 9.5% decrease in grades. These findings suggest that education in a non-native language presents significant challenges and additional educational burdens. Speciale (2012) explored the link between immigration, ethnic diversity, and public goods provision, revealing that a rise in the immigrant population marginally reduces public education spending, especially in the context of Tiebout-type migration. This indicates an extra educational burden from immigrant admissions.[5] Zinovyeva et al. (2014) also observed that the performance of immigrant children improves over time in the host

Yasuoka (2024) focused on the impacts of these differences. While such perspectives are indeed important, this chapter concentrates on elucidating the long-term effects on generational welfare through pension finances.

[3] Valbuena et al. (2021) also determined that grade retention is likely an inefficient policy, noting that the associated costs can easily surpass any potential benefits. They recommend replacing it with a more effective alternative.

[4] The OECD (2013) highlighted that, besides Japan, only Malaysia and Norway have not adopted a grade repetition system.

[5] Casarico and Devillanova (2003) and Mavisakalyan (2011) have shown that immigrants' influence on private educational decisions is significant in the context of human capital development. Nonetheless, for simplicity, this chapter focuses solely on the structural effects resulting from immigration.

country, highlighting the need for additional government support, such as language assistance.

The inclusion of immigrant workers influences native welfare via direct wage impacts, the economic burden of educating their children, and the PAYG pension system. In their study on immigration's effect on educational needs in host countries, Jinno and Yasuoka (2022) overlooked the potential advantages for native residents stemming from immigrants' contributions to the PAYG pension system.[6]

Razin and Sadka (1999, 2000) explored how the admission of unskilled immigrant workers impacts the welfare of both low-skilled and high-skilled native workers within the PAYG system. Notably, Razin and Sadka (2000) identified negative net benefits from accepting immigrants in economies without access to international capital markets, as demonstrated through numerical analysis. Although the model differentiates between skilled and unskilled workers primarily by their labor supply, both immigrant and native workers are considered perfectly substitutable. Consequently, the introduction of immigrants implicitly reduces the wage rate and capital-labor ratio, adversely affecting native welfare. These outcomes are based on the premise of perfect substitutability between native and immigrant labor and the absence of additional educational costs for immigrant children. However, these findings could vary with changes in the level of substitutability and the expenses associated with educating immigrant children. In a manner akin to Razin and Sadka (2000), we conduct a numerical analysis with specific values to explore the dynamics of how accepting foreign workers impacts the wages of native residents and their overall welfare. This analysis aims to provide a detailed understanding of the economic consequences of foreign worker admission on the native population.[7]

There exists a variety of PAYG pension systems, each with its unique response to immigration. Therefore, we will focus on three key systems: the Defined Contribution (DC), the Defined Benefit (DB), and the Defined Rate (DR) pension systems. Our objective is to comparatively analyze the impacts of immigrant admission in Japan through these systems. This analysis will be conducted in the context of Japan's economic landscape, characterized by imperfect substitutability between immigrant and native labor, along with the added educational burden of immigrant children.[8]

---

[6] Jinno and Yasuoka (2022) found that immigration can enhance the welfare of native residents if the need for extra educators for immigrant children is minimal. However, their analysis using Japanese data indicates that the benefits of admitting immigrants do not outweigh the drawbacks, thus not improving the welfare of Japanese natives. Kemnitz (2003) explored how immigration affects a host country with a welfare state that supports both unemployed and elderly populations, based on the premise that immigrant and native labor are perfectly substitutable.

[7] Razin and Sadka (1999) assumed that the children of foreign workers could assimilate into the host country without any burden and exhibit the same productivity as natives. Jinno (2011, 2013) analyzed the impact (net benefits) on pension finances of accepting unskilled workers, assuming that additional costs are necessary for the children of foreign workers to reach the same productivity as natives once they become adults. However, these analyses also assumed complete substitutability of unskilled workers, unlike the imperfect substitutability considered in this paper.

[8] Casarico and Devillanova (2003) and Brunello et al. (2020) examined the impact of immigration on the self-driven accumulation of human capital among native populations. Their research indicated that natives tend to enhance their human capital accumulation in response to immigration. Although

In this chapter, we compare the impact of immigrant admission on the wages and welfare of both natives and immigrants through numerical analysis in Japan, a country facing significant aging and expected increases in social security spending, particularly on pensions. Admitting immigrants could potentially alleviate the fiscal burden on future generations. Previous studies, such as those by Shimasawa and Oguro (2010), Imrohoroğlu, Kitao, and Yamada (2017), and Okamoto (2021), have examined the quantitative effects of immigrant admission in Japan using overlapping-generations simulation models, suggesting that it reduces the financial load on future generations.[9] However, these studies did not take into account the production relationship between natives and immigrants, i.e., whether they are substitutes or complements, which is an aspect this chapter addresses.

The structure of this chapter is as follows: Sect. 2 provides a brief overview of the history and current situation of foreign workers in Japan. Sections 3 and 4 detail the model and welfare analysis, respectively. Section 5 discusses the findings, and Sect. 6 concludes the chapter.

2 Brief History and Current Situation of Foreign Students and Workers in Japan

Japan has historically faced challenges in educating foreign students within its "no grade repetition" system, addressing these issues by allocating funds to hire extra teachers. Oh (2019) highlighted that although many Koreans returned to their homeland post-war, approximately 600,000 remained in Japan due to the Korean peninsula's instability, severe restrictions on property transfer out of Japan, and their established livelihoods in Japan. The revision of the Immigration Control Law and Refugee Recognition Act in 1989,[10] which facilitated the entry of Japanese descendants and

---

this chapter acknowledges the extra burden on natives due to the education of immigrant children, it does not delve into natives' endogenous responses, such as increased human capital formation, to maintain computational simplicity. Addressing this aspect remains a topic for future research.

[9] Shimasawa and Oguro (2010) researched the impact of an immigration policy permitting a constant influx of 150,000 immigrants annually on Japan's fiscal burden. Their findings indicated a slight reduction in the debt-to-GDP ratio compared to a baseline scenario without immigration. Imrohoroğlu, Kitao, and Yamada (2017) delved into the consequences of accepting guest workers, who were ineligible for public pensions, on fiscal sustainability. Their study concluded that such programs could alleviate Japan's fiscal challenges. Okamoto (2021) investigated the implications of an immigration policy with varying durations and endogenous fertility under a fixed total number of immigrants, identifying the optimal length for such a policy. Other research examining the influence of immigration on public finances includes work by Lee and Miller (2000), Storesletten (2000), Auerbach and Oreopoulos (2000), and Collado, Iturbe-Ormaetxe, and Valera (2004). These studies commonly suggest that the admission of medium- or high-skilled immigrants eases the fiscal load on future native populations. However, a notable limitation in these analyses is the assumption of perfect substitutability between natives and immigrants, who are categorized as having equivalent education and experience.

[10] Please see the detail of the law at Japanese Law Transformation (n.d.).

Table 1 Number of foreign residents in Japan by status of residence, 31 December 2022

Statuses of residence and visas for foreigners in Japan	Number
Residence statuses for foreigners based on their activities (except foreign workers with specific skills or technical intern training)	452,732
Foreign workers with specific skills or technical intern training	455,863
Statuses of residence for foreigners based on status or position	1,551,846
Others	614,772

Source: Immigration Services Agency of Japan, "Statistics on Foreign Residents" (Table 22–12-t1, as of 31 Dec 2022; published 7 July 2023), Ministry of Justice, e-Stat[in Japanese]. Retrieved 30 June 2025 from https://www.e-stat.go.jp/stat-search/files?page=1&layout=dataset&toukei=00250012&tstat=000001018034&tclass1=000001060399

their families to mitigate labor shortages, and the introduction in 2019 of a system allowing "Foreign technical interns" to change their status to "Special skilled workers" who can bring their families, have accentuated the challenge of educating foreign children in Japan.[11] Consequently, Japan has increasingly welcomed foreign workers from abroad. Table 1 displays the number of foreigners in Japan by residence status as of December 2022.

Currently, precise details on the final educational backgrounds of foreigners in Japan are not fully available. However, in a survey by the Immigration Services Agency of Japan, conducted from February 18 to March 3 in Reiwa Year 4 2022, which received 7,982 valid responses out of 40,000 distributed questionnaires, it was found that 56.1% of the respondents had attained an education level of vocational school, junior college, or lower in their home country. This was the highest level of education for this group. Conversely, 39.7% of the respondents held a university or graduate degree. These figures suggest a relatively high proportion of individuals with lower educational levels among the respondents.[12]

Since its establishment, education for foreign children in Japan has often been regarded more as a privilege than a compulsory service. This perspective has led to issues like low enrollment rates and insufficient academic support. Reflecting the contemporary scenario, as of 2021, the total number of students needing Japanese language instruction climbed to 58,307, according to a report by the Ministry of

[11] The Ministry of Education, Culture, Sports, Science and Technology (MEXT) in Japan is undertaking a survey on the enrollment of students, irrespective of nationality, who require Japanese language instruction in public elementary, junior high, and high schools. This initiative aims to enhance the educational support for children needing Japanese language lessons. In 2021, the total count of foreign students requiring Japanese language instruction reached 58,307, with the number of foreign students at 47,619. This represents an increase of 6,864 students (16.8% higher) compared to the previous survey. For more detailed information, please visit MEXT's website. Note that the website is in Japanese.

[12] Source: Immigration Services Agency of Japan, Basic Survey on Foreign Residents, FY 2022 (fieldwork: 18 Feb – 3 Mar 2023), Ministry of Justice, Tokyo [in Japanese]. Retrieved 30 June 2025 from https://www.moj.go.jp/isa/content/001402047.pdf.

Education, Culture, Sports, Science and Technology (2023).[13] For the fiscal year 2023, the allocated budget for Foreign National Coexistence Policies totaled 177.5 billion yen. A portion of this budget was dedicated to personnel expenses, which include the cost of hiring additional teachers, to support students who require Japanese language instruction. This allocation represented a 12.5% increase from the previous year's budget.[14]

Until recent years, there were no public statistics from surveys focusing on nationality in Japan, except for a few instances like the "National Census." The absence of income data in the "National Census" made it challenging to analyze the relationship between nationality and income levels in the country.[15] It was only recently, beginning with the 2019 Basic Survey on Wage Structure (BSWS) conducted by the Ministry of Health, Labor, and Welfare (2020), that Japan started to systematically collect and analyze data on nationality in conjunction with income levels.[16]

The latest version of the 2020 Basic Survey on Wage Structure (BSWS) provides a comprehensive overview of the average income level of all workers, as detailed in the Ministry of Health, Labor, and Welfare (2021) report. Table 2 summarizes this data. The 2020 BSWS data was derived from 54,874 valid responses out of 78,181 targeted establishments, of which 48,007 were private establishments with 10 or more regular employees.

The 2020 Basic Survey on Wage Structure (BSWS) provides key insights into foreign workers in Japan. These workers are typically younger and have shorter tenures compared to their native counterparts. Moreover, their average monthly contractual cash earnings are significantly lower and distributed differently than those of native workers. While this data suggests that the effective productivity of foreign workers may be lower than that of native workers, the exact nature of their relationship remains uncertain.

Consequently, in the next section, we will develop a model that integrates the dynamics between foreign and native workers. Following this, we will perform a

---

[13] The total number of students in need of Japanese language instruction comprises not only foreign-born children but also Japanese nationals who require such support.

[14] Source (Japanese): Immigration Services Agency of Japan, *Comprehensive Policy for the Acceptance and Coexistence of Foreign Workers* (https://www.moj.go.jp/isa/support/coexistence/04_00019.html, accessed 30 June 2025).

[15] A limited number of studies, such as those by Nakamura, Naito, Kambayashi, Kawaguchi, and Machikita (2009) and Kosaki (2018), have explored the impact of admitting foreign workers on the wages of native workers. These studies utilized the ratio of foreigners to natives in local areas as reported in the "National Census."

[16] Currently, Korekawa (2023) represents the sole analysis in Japan that has utilized microdata on nationality and income level from the Basic Survey on Wage Structure (BSWS). This study revealed that the status of residence negatively impacts income levels. However, it did not examine the relationship between native and foreign workers in terms of the production function, as conducted by Guerreiro et al. (2020) and Llull (2020). Consequently, the degree of substitutability between native and foreign workers remains unclear. Our aim is to explore the impact of admitting foreign workers on the welfare of natives within the economic structure, particularly through the production function. This is why we have chosen to use simulation analysis to assess their effects, assuming various degrees of substitutability between them.

Table 2 Comparison between foreign workers and native workers

	Foreign workers	Native workers
Average age	33.3	43.2
Average length of service (year)	2.7	11.9
Average monthly contractual cash earnings (thousand yen)	218.1	307.7
Total number	39,745	27,650,230

Note In our analysis, we utilized the frequency table from the Basic Survey on Wage Structure (BSWS, 2020) and conducted an F-test and a Welch t-test to compare the variances and means of the two groups under study. The F-statistic was calculated to be 0.66388, with a p-value of less than 0.00. Similarly, the t-statistic was found to be − 144.39, also with a p-value of less than 0.00. Based on these results, we can reject the null hypothesis, which posits that the variances of the two groups are equal and that their means are the same

simulation analysis to assess the impacts of admitting foreign workers. This analysis will be grounded in various assumptions regarding their imperfect substitutability.

3 The Model

The model we are utilizing, devised by Jinno and Yasuoka (2022), acknowledges the imperfect substitutability between natives and immigrants and examines different pension systems in a full employment scenario.

In this model, we apply an overlapping generations framework where individuals pass through three life stages: childhood, the working period, and retirement. Education is a necessity during childhood. During the working period, natives are endowed with a single unit of labor, which they supply inelastically to either the consumption or education sectors. Immigrants, also in their working period, allocate a portion of their labor endowment to the consumption sector. It is critical to note that natives and immigrants are not perfectly substitutable in the consumption sector. Individuals make choices concerning their consumption, savings, and the number of children they plan to have. Following these decisions, they enter retirement, living off their savings and pension benefits.

In this context, "immigrant" refers specifically to individuals admitted as non-citizens in the initial period. To simplify, we assume that the productivity of immigrant children is equivalent to that of native children, thanks to the educational support provided by additional educators. Therefore, in the following period, these immigrant children are considered as natives.

3.1 Admitting Immigrants in the Working Period

In each period of the model, λ_t represents the rate of native workers during period t. This is set against the backdrop of a continuous influx of immigrant workers into the country, who enter without capital. This dynamic is crucial for understanding the changing composition of the workforce and its impact on the economy over time.

$$N_t^{IM} = \lambda_t N_t^N, \tag{1}$$

where N_t^{IM} denotes the number of immigrants in period t, and N_t^N represents the number of native working individuals in period t. The superscripts IM and N are used to distinguish between immigrants and native residents, respectively. Consequently, the total population of the tth generation, including both immigrants and natives, is expressed as $N_t^T = N_t^N + N_t^{IM} = (1 + \lambda_t)N_t^N$. P represents the relative productivity of immigrant workers compared to their native counterparts. In our mode, we assume that P is less than 1, indicating that the productivity of immigrants is considered to be lower than that of the native workers.[17]

3.2 Child-Rearing and Education

In our model, the native population's children require a specific number of educators for upbringing and education, denoted as h^N. However, the children of immigrants necessitate additional educators, leading to the requirement that h^{IM}, the number of educators for immigrant children, be greater than h^N. This reflects the additional educational needs of immigrant children. Therefore, the relationship between the number of educators per child for natives and immigrants is established as follows:

$$h^N < h^{IM} = qh^N \tag{2}$$

where $q > 1$. This differential in educational support underscores the additional resources required to effectively educate children from immigrant backgrounds.

In period t, the total number of educators required for both native and immigrant children, denoted as H_t, is calculated as $H_t = h^N n_t^N + h^{IM} n_t^{IM}$. Here, n_t^N represents the number of children per native worker, while n_t^{IM} represents the number of children per immigrant worker. It is assumed that only natives are employed as educators, as they are responsible for teaching both immigrant and native children the language,

[17] Jinno and Yasuoka (2022), drawing on data from the Basic Survey on Wage Structure (BSWS) conducted by the Ministry of Health, Labor, and Welfare (Ministry of Health, Labour, and Welfare, 2021), determined that in Japan, the relative productivity of immigrants compared to natives is 0.61. This figure, being less than 1, indicates that immigrants' productivity is lower than that of native workers. For more comprehensive information and context, please refer to Jinno and Yasuoka (2022).

culture, and other essential skills of the host country. Using Eqs. (1) and (2), the number of educators can be calculated as follows:

$$H_t^N = \left(n_t^N + \lambda_t q \bullet n_t^{IM}\right)h^N N_t^N. \tag{3}$$

Given the provision of a sufficient number of educators, immigrant children are enabled to fully develop their abilities, achieving a level comparable to that of native children by the time they reach adulthood.[18] For the sake of simplicity in our model, we treat immigrant children as natives in the subsequent period, $t+1$. Therefore, the generational population transition, including immigrants, is formulated as follows:

$$N_{t+1}^N = n_t^N N_t^N + n_t^{IM} N_t^{IM} \tag{4}$$

The population in period $t+1$ is a function of the number of children born to both native and immigrant workers in period t, who are now regarded as natives in period $t+1$. This approach assumes that with adequate educational support, the children of immigrants seamlessly integrate and contribute to the native population in the next generation.

Using Eq. (1), the transition of the generation's population from Eq. (4) is as follows:

$$\frac{N_{t+1}^N}{N_t^N} = \overline{n}_t^N = \left(n_t^N + \lambda_t n_t^{IM}\right) \tag{4'}$$

where $\overline{n}_t^N$ represents the average population growth rate of natives, which encompasses immigrant children as well. This inclusion is based on the assumption that immigrant children, once educated, reach a productivity level comparable to that of native children by adulthood. Therefore, the growth rate in Eq. (4) is interpreted from a productivity standpoint.

3.3 *Firms in the Consumption Sector*

The production function is $Y_t^T = \left(K_t^T\right)^{\delta}\left(L_t^T\right)^{(1-\delta)}$, where $\delta \in (0, 1)$. Y_t, K_t, and L_t denote output produced, capital, and labor, respectively. The variables with superscript T represent the total number of variables (e.g., capital or labor). To examine the relationship between natives and immigrants, potentially characterized by either perfect or imperfect substitution (or complementarity), we utilize the following

[18] The assumption made here is quite strong. According to the OECD's 2019 PISA results (OECD 2019), immigrant children's scores are generally lower than those of native children, despite receiving more educational support in some host countries. This observation aligns with Jinno's findings (2011, 2013), suggesting that the additional challenge of assimilating into the host country warrants explicit consideration, an aspect outside the scope of this chapter.

production function.[19] The total labor supply is denoted as follows:

$$L_t^T = \left[\psi\left(L_t^N\right)^{\phi} + (1-\psi)\left(L_t^{IM}\right)^{\phi}\right]^{\frac{1}{\phi}}, \quad if\ \phi \leq 1,\ or\ \phi \neq 0\ or$$
$$L_t^T = \left(L_t^N\right)^{\psi}\left(L_t^{IM}\right)^{1-\psi}, \quad if\ \phi = 0, \tag{5}$$

where $L_t^N\left(L_t^{IM}\right)$ is the labor force supplied by natives (immigrants). The relationship between natives and immigrants becomes perfectly substitutable when $\phi = 1$. The relationship between natives and immigrants becomes an imperfect substitute when $0 < \phi < 1$. The relationship between natives and immigrants becomes complementary when $\phi < 0$. Subsequently, we assume that $\phi \neq 0$. $K_t^T = s_t^N N_t^N + s_t^{IM} N_t^{IM}$, where s_t^X $(X = NorIM)$ is the amount of savings per native or immigrant.

We assume that all capital depreciates at the end of each period. In line with the theory of profit maximization, this leads to the following conclusion:

$$(1+r_t) = \delta\left(k_t^N\right)^{\delta-1}\left[\psi\left(\epsilon_t^N\right)^{\phi} + (1-\psi)(\lambda_t \mathrm{P})^{\phi}\right]^{\frac{1-\delta}{\phi}} \tag{6-a}$$

$$w_t^N = (1-\delta)\psi\left(k_t^N\right)^{\delta}\left[\psi\left(\epsilon_t^N\right)^{\phi} + (1-\psi)(\lambda_t \mathrm{P})^{\phi}\right]^{\frac{1-\delta-\phi}{\phi}}\left(\epsilon_t^N\right)^{\phi-1} \tag{6-b}$$

$$w_t^{IM} = (1-\delta)(1-\psi)\left(k_t^N\right)^{\delta}\left[\psi\left(\epsilon_t^N\right)^{\phi} + (1-\psi)(\lambda_t \mathrm{P})^{\phi}\right]^{\frac{1-\delta-\phi}{\phi}}(\lambda_t \mathrm{P})^{\phi-1} \tag{6-c}$$

where ϵ_t^N represents the ratio of native employees in the consumption sector, defined as $\frac{E_t^N}{N_t^N}$, with E_t^N being the number of natives employed in this sector. This ratio can be computed using Eq. (3) as follows:

$$\epsilon_t^N = 1 - \left(n_t^N + \lambda_t q n_t^{IM}\right)h^N \tag{7}$$

We obtain the following relationships by logarithmically differentiating Eqs. (6-b) and (6-c) to L_t^{IM} and L_t^N, respectively, as follows:

$$\frac{d\ln w_t^N}{d\ln L_t^{IM}} \gtrless 0 \text{and} \frac{d\ln w_t^{IM}}{d\ln L_t^N} \gtrless 0 \quad \text{if } \phi \lesseqgtr (1-\delta) \tag{8}$$

Thus, if $1-\delta \leq \phi < 1$, the relationship between natives and immigrants is imperfectly substitutable. In this scenario, an increase in the number of immigrants (natives) leads to a decrease in the wage rate of natives (immigrants). Conversely, if $0 < \phi < 1-\delta$, the relationship remains imperfectly substitutable, but here, an increase in the number of immigrants (natives) results in an increase in the wage rate of natives (immigrants). Finally, if $\phi < 0$, the relationship between natives

[19] This formula for the production function was adapted from Llull (2020), who investigated the impact of immigration on productivity.

and immigrants is complementary, where an increase in the number of immigrants (natives) enhances the wage rate of the natives (immigrants).[20]

Using Eqs. (6-b) and (6-c), we calculate the relative wage rate as follows:

$$\frac{w_t^{IM}}{w_t^N} = \Psi\left(\chi_t^E\right)^{1-\phi} \tag{9}$$

where $\chi_t = \frac{\epsilon_t^N}{\lambda_t \mathrm{P}}$ and $\Psi = \frac{(1-\psi)}{\psi}$. The average income among natives and immigrants, $\overline{w}_t = \frac{w_t^N N_t^N + w_t^{IM} P N_t^{IM}}{N_t^N + N_t^{IM}}$, becomes

$$\overline{w}_t = \left(\frac{w_t^N + \lambda_t P w_t^{IM}}{1 + \lambda_t}\right) \tag{10}$$

by using Eq. (1).

3.4 *Education Sector*

Educator wages are covered by the shared educational costs for both natives and immigrants, indicated as z_t^E. Variables with an E superscript are applicable to both natives and immigrants. The budget constraint for educational expenses is expressed as $z_t^E\left(n_t^N N_t^N + n_t^{IM} N_t^{IM}\right) = w_t^{edu} H_t^N$, where w_t^{edu} represents the wage rate for educators. Natives have the option to serve as educators in the education sector or as workers in the consumption sector. Because natives freely move between these sectors, the wage rate for educators aligns with that of workers, resulting in $w_t^N = w_t^{edu}$.

Thus, using Eqs. (1) and (2) and considering the arbitrage movement caused by the natives, the education expenses become

$$z_t^E = \left(\frac{n_t^N + \lambda_t q n_t^{IM}}{n_t^N + \lambda_t n_t^{IM}}\right) w_t^N h^N. \tag{11}$$

An increase in the value of q leads to higher education expenses. Consequently, admitting immigrants whose children place a relatively larger burden on the education system results in increased educational costs.

---

[20] In a small open economy context, capital supply is modeled as $1 + r_t = (K_t)^{\kappa}$, where $\left(\frac{1}{k}\right)$ denotes the capital supply elasticity, as discussed in Dustmann et al. (2016) and Llull (2020). Integrating this elasticity and Eq. (6-a) into Eq. (6-b), and then differentiating the wages of natives with respect to L_t^{IM}, yields the condition in Eq. (8): $\phi \lesseqgtr \frac{(1+\kappa)(1-\alpha)}{1-\alpha+\kappa}$. This formulation is more straightforward than that in Llull (2020), which involves differentiating native wages in relation to the immigrant-to-native ratio. A larger capital supply elasticity (smaller κ) reduces the value of $\frac{(1+\kappa)(1-\alpha)}{1-\alpha+\kappa}$. If $\kappa - 0$ (indicating perfectly elastic capital supply), Eq. (8) simplifies to $\phi \lesseqgtr 1$, suggesting that imperfectly substitutable immigrants enhance native wages. This outcome contrasts with Razin and Sadka (2000), who assume perfect substitutability between natives and immigrants.

3.5 The Pension System

Three types of pension systems are considered herein.

3.5.1 A Pension System with a Defined Contribution Rate: The DC Pension System

The primary pension model is the defined contribution rate system. In this system, the pension premium remains fixed, and the accumulated pension contributions are evenly distributed among the elderly as pension benefits. The average pension benefit is determined endogenously.

The budget constraint for this pension system is outlined below:

$$pen_{t+1}^{E}N_{t}^{N}+pen_{t+1}^{E}N_{t}^{IM}=\theta^{E}w_{t+1}^{N}N_{t+1}^{N}+\theta^{E}w_{t+1}^{IM}\mathrm{P}N_{t+1}^{IM} \tag{12-a}$$

where pen_{t+1}^{E} is the common pension benefit for the old in the $t+1$st period, and θ^{E} is the exogenously defined contribution rate.

By substituting Eqs. (1), (4), and (9) into Eq. (12-a), we obtain the endogenously determined pension benefit as follows:

$$pen_{t+1}^{E}=\left(\frac{1+\lambda_{t+1}}{1+\lambda_{t}}\right)\theta^{E}\overline{n}_{t}^{N}\overline{w}_{t+1} \tag{13-a}$$

We have a replacement ratio in period $t+1$: $v_{t+1}\equiv\frac{pen_{t+1}^{E}}{\overline{w}_{t+1}}=\left(\frac{1+\lambda_{t+1}}{1+\lambda_{t}}\right)\theta^{E}\overline{n}_{t}$ from Eq. (13-a).

3.5.2 A Pension System with a Defined Benefit: The DB Pension System

In this system, the pension benefit remains constant, leading to the endogenous determination of the pension contribution required to meet the budget constraint of the pension system, which is specified as follows:

$$pen^{E}N_{t}^{N}+pen^{E}N_{t}^{IM}=\theta_{t+1}^{E}w_{t+1}^{N}N_{t+1}^{N}+\theta_{t+1}^{E}w_{t+1}^{IM}N_{t+1}^{IM} \tag{12-b}$$

By substituting Eqs. (1) and (4) into Eq. (12-b), we obtain the endogenously determined pension contribution as follows:

$$\theta_{t+1}^{E}=\left(\frac{1+\lambda_{t}}{1+\lambda_{t+1}}\right)\frac{pen^{E}}{\overline{n}_{t}^{N}\overline{w}_{t+1}} \tag{13-b}$$

3.5.3 A Pension System with a Defined Pension Replacement Rate: The DR Pension System

In this system, the pension benefit is adjusted to a specific rate of the average income of the working generation: $\overline{pen}_{t+1} = v\overline{w}_{t+1}$, where v represents the income replacement rate. The contribution rate is endogenously determined to fund the budget constraint, which is described as follows:

$$pen_{t+1}^{E} N_t^{N} + pen_{t+1}^{E} N_t^{IM} = \theta_{t+1}^{E} w_{t+1}^{N} N_{t+1}^{N} + \theta_{t+1}^{E} w_{t+1}^{IM} \mathrm{P} N_{t+1}^{IM} \tag{12-c}$$

By substituting Eqs. (1) and (4'), and $\overline{pen}_{t+1} = v^E \overline{w}_{t+1}$ into Eq. (12-c), we obtain the endogenously determined pension contribution rate as follows:

$$\theta_{t+1}^{E} = \left(\frac{1+\lambda_t}{1+\lambda_{t+1}} \right) \frac{v^E}{\overline{n}_t^N} \tag{13-c}$$

3.6 *Consumption Utility*

The utility of individuals is based on the quantity of consumer goods they consume in their youth and old age, as well as the number of children they have. Their utility function is outlined as follows:

$$U_t^X = \alpha \ln c_t^X + \beta \ln d_{t+1}^X + \gamma \ln n_t^X, \tag{14}$$

where $\alpha + \beta + \gamma = 1$, and $X = N$ or IM. The budget constraints for the young and old individuals are as follows:

$$c_t^X + z_t^E n_t^X + s_t^X = \left(1 - \theta_t^E\right) In_t^X, \quad \text{and} \tag{15}$$

$$d_{t+1}^X = (1 + r_{t+1}) s_t^X + pen_{t+1}^E \tag{16}$$

where $X = N$ or IM, and $In_t^N = w_t^N$ and $In_t^{IM} = \mathrm{P} w_t^{IM}$.

Individuals determine the optimal savings and number of children during their working years to maximize their utility. Through certain calculations, the following optimal solutions are derived:

$$s_t^{X*} = \frac{\beta(1-\theta) In_t^X \bullet R_{t+1} - (1-\beta) pen_{t+1}^X}{R_{t+1}}, \tag{17}$$

$$n_t^{X*} = \gamma \frac{(1-\theta) In_t^X \bullet R_{t+1} + pen_{t+1}^X}{z_t \bullet R_{t+1}}. \tag{18}$$

Capital accumulation is $K_{t+1} = s_t^{N^*} N_t^N + s_t^{IM^*} N_t^{IM}$, where capital is perfectly depleted in one period. Capital per native $\left(k_{t+1}^N\right)$ is calculated as follows:

$$k_{t+1}^N = \frac{s_t^{N^*} + \lambda s_t^{IM^*}}{n_t^{N^*} + \lambda n_t^{IM^*}}. \tag{19}$$

We possess all the necessary variables to assess the impact of immigrants. In the following section, we will explore the effects of increasing immigrant numbers on the welfare of both native and immigrant generations. This analysis will be conducted through simulation, considering various pension systems.

4 Simulation Analysis

In this section, we conduct a simulation to analyze the effects of increasing the admission of immigrants from 2 to 10%, utilizing Fortran for the computational analysis. The crucial exogenous parameters are outlined in Table 3.

We concentrate on certain calculations regarding the parameters listed in Table 1. The subjective discount rate per year is assumed to be exp(− 0.01). With the assumption that one period equals 30 years, the subjective discount rate for each period is calculated as 0.741. Productivity per working hour is defined as the quotient of scheduled cash earnings and the actual number of hours worked, information that is available from the BSWS released by the Ministry of Health, Labour, and Welfare (2021). The respective values for natives and immigrants are 2.061 and 1.659. Consequently, this leads to a ratio of 0.805, which is utilized as the value of P. The annual income is determined by multiplying scheduled cash earnings by 12 and then adding the annual special cash earnings. This calculation results in an average annual income of 4.965 million yen for natives and 3.651 million yen for immigrants. Consequently, the ratio of the average annual income of natives to that of immigrants is established at 1.786. To get the value, the value of ψ is adjusted. Dividing the total number of

Table 3 Key parameters

Key parameter	Value	Key parameter	Value
α	0.548	ψ	0.750
β	0.741 α	h^N	0.062
γ	$1 - \alpha - \beta$	q	1.506
δ	0.499	θ	0.183
P	0.805		

Note The preferences from α to γ are adjusted to get the fertility rate as 0.65 per capita. The value of δ is obtained from Japan Institute for Labour Policy and Training (2023), and it is calculated by dividing the labor costs by the total added value. The contribution rate of the welfare pension system in Japan is 0.183

Table 4 The value of ϕ

Case	Relationship	Value of ϕ
(A)	perfectly substitutable decreasing the wage rate of natives	1.0
(B)	imperfectly substitutable decreasing the wage rate of natives	0.82
(C)	imperfectly substitutable increasing the wage rate of natives	0.52
(D)	complementary increasing the wage rate of natives	– 0.05

Note The value of ϕ represents the relationship between natives and immigrants

faculty members by the total number of students, as reported in the Statistics Abstract of Education (MEXT, 2022), results in a ratio of 0.102, which is h^N. Aichi Prefecture, known for having one of the largest populations of foreign workers and the most advanced education system for foreign children in Japan, serves as a key example in our study. To assess the most comprehensive educational burden, we adopt the value of q based on the scenario in Aichi Prefecture for this paper.[21]

The ideal approach for this analysis would involve estimating values directly from data; however, due to data limitations, this is not practicable. Consequently, we resort to using representative values based on reasonable assumptions. These values are then employed to simulate the impact of immigration on the economy and the welfare of natives.

We utilize the representative values for the relationship between natives and immigrants as shown in Table 4. With these key parameters, our simulation explores the effects of increasing the admission of immigrants from 2 to 10% in the third period, followed by a return to the original level in subsequent periods.[22] We obtain the steady-state values in the case that $\phi = 0.82$, which are listed in Table 3.[23] Immigrants are presumed to evolve from being perfectly substitutable to becoming complementary to natives. However, they are considered to be perfectly substitutable with other immigrants who have already settled in the host country when new immigrants are admitted.

---

[21] For the details of the derivation method on the value of q, please refer to Jinno and Yasuoka (2022).

[22] As of the end of October 2020, according to the "Foreign Employment Status" published by the Ministry of Health, Labour, and Welfare (2021), there are approximately 1,724 thousand immigrant workers in Japan. The "Labor Force Survey" (2021) by Ministry of Health, Labour, and Welfare reports the total number of workers in Japan around that time as about 66.94 million. This places the current rate of immigrant workers at approximately 2%. We start our analysis with an initial immigration rate of 2%. However, if the relationship between natives and immigrants is complementary, this rate of immigration may be too low to effectively estimate the impacts of admitting more immigrants. Therefore, we also calculate the effects of admitting immigrants at a higher rate of 5%, assuming an initial immigration rate of 10%.

[23] The steady-state values vary depending on the value of ϕ. However, these variations are not crucial for our analysis. In this paper, we will focus on describing only the essential points of difference.

Table 5 Endogenously calculated variables at the steady state of this model with $\phi = 0.82$

Endogenous variable	Value	Endogenous variable	Value	Endogenous variable	Value
k^*	0.039	n_*^N	0.648	u_*^N	– 2.901
$1+r^*$	2.103	n_*^{IM}	0.381	u_*^{IM}	– 3.640
w_*^N	0.084	s_*^N	0.025	pen_*^E	0.010
$P \bullet w_*^{IM}$	0.047	s_*^{IM}	0.013	v_*^E	0.120
		ϵ_*^N	0.959	z_*^E	0.052

Note These endogenous variables change depending on the value of ϕ. The endogenous variables at the initial steady state are the same among the different pension systems when the value of ϕ is the same.[a] In the case of (A) and (B), the endogenously calculated variables are reasonable because the wage rate of the natives is higher than that of the immigrants, which exactly describes the current situation in Japan[b]

[a] When the value of ϕ is between 1.0 and 0.8, which satisfies the condition $(1-\delta) < \phi$, an increase in the number of immigrants (natives) decreases the wage rate of the natives (immigrants). Conversely, when the value of ϕ is between 0.65 and – 0.03, which satisfies the condition $(1-\delta) > \phi$, an increase in the number of immigrants (natives) increases the wage rate of the natives (immigrants)

[b] Research indicates that immigrant women generally have higher fertility rates than native women in many developed countries. However, contrary to these trends, it has been found that the fertility rates of immigrant women in Japan are lower than those of Japanese women. Korekawa (2023) explores the reasons behind this lower fertility rate among immigrant women in Japan

4.1 Comparisons

We now evaluate the impact of admitting additional immigrants under a general PAYG pension system, applying Eqs. (13-a), (13-b), and (13-c). In this context, admitting more immigrants increases the number of individuals in the working generation who collectively support pension benefits. The simulation outcomes for admitting more immigrants are detailed in Tables 6-a, 6-b, 7-a and 7-b.

Additionally, we assess the effects on immigrant wages and utility when considering the defined contribution rate of the PAYG pension system (the DC pension system). This analysis involves using Eq. (12-a) as the budget constraint for the pension system. The results of these effects are displayed in Tables 6-a and 6-b.

As indicated in Tables 6-a and 6-b, the impact of admitting more immigrants on the wages and utility of natives turns negative (positive) when immigrants are relatively more substitutable (complementary) with natives.

We direct our attention to Cases (A) and (B), which illustrate the effects of admitting perfectly or imperfectly substitutable immigrants within a stable steady-state economy. In both of these cases, the total utility changes are negative, despite the reduction in natives' wage rates following immigrant admissions. In contrast, for Cases (C) and (D), the total utility change is positive, even though there is no alteration in the utility level of natives with the admission of immigrants. This observation underscores the critical importance of the parameter condition—whether the admission of immigrants increases or does not increase the wages of natives—especially when an economy incorporates immigrants under the DC pension system.

Table 6-a The effects of admitting immigrants on the wages and utility of natives under the DC pension system

Natives								
	(A) $\phi =$ 1.00		(B) $\phi =$ 0.82		(C) $\phi =$ 0.52		(D) $\phi =$ – 0.05	
Total utility change		– 0.608%		– 0.452%		0.737%		3.374%
	Wage (%)	Utility (%)	Wage (%)	Utility (%)	Wage (%)	Utility (%)	Wage (%)	Utility (%)
1	0.00	0.000	0.00	0.00	0.00	0.00	0.00	0.00
2	0.00	0.072	0.00	0.17	0.00	0.50	0.00	1.96
3	**– 1.02**	**– 0.4419**	**– 1.05**	**– 0.49**	**0.27**	**0.00**	**35.71**	**0.00**
4	– 0.50	– 0.239	– 0.28	– 0.14	0.53	0.24	4.38	1.41
5	0.00	0.000	0.00	0.00	0.00	0.00	0.00	0.00
6	0.00	0.000	0.00	0.00	0.00	0.00	0.00	0.00
7	0.00	0.000	0.00	0.00	0.00	0.00	0.00	0.00
8	0.00	0.000	0.00	0.00	0.00	0.00	0.00	0.00
9	0.00	0.000	0.00	0.00	0.00	0.00	0.00	0.00
10	0.00	0.000	0.00	0.00	0.00	0.00	0.00	0.00

Notes The first column in above table represents generations. The subsequent values indicate the wages and utilities of these generations, calculated as deviation rates from the initial steady state. A positive (negative) value signifies an improvement (deterioration) in their respective measures when foreign workers are admitted in the third period, which is indicated in bold. To the right of the "total utility change" column, we show the sum of the deviation rates for each period, calculated without discounting. These explanatory notes are also applicable to Tables 6-a, 6-b, 7-a, 7-b, 8-a, 8-b

Similarly, in Cases (A) and (B), the total utility changes are negative, despite a decrease in the wage rate of immigrants when more are admitted. However, in Cases (C) and (D), the total utility change is positive, even though there is a decrease in the wage rate and no change in the utility level of immigrants upon admitting more immigrants.

We also evaluate the impact of admitting more immigrants on their wages and utility in the context of the defined benefits of the PAYG pension system (the DB pension system). This analysis uses Eq. (12-b) as the budget constraint of the pension system. These effects are detailed in Tables 7-a and 7-b.

Under the DB pension system, the fundamental results mirror those under the DC pension system. If the condition of the parameters satisfies $(1-\delta) < \phi$, then the total utility changes for both natives and immigrants turn negative. Conversely, when $(1-\delta) > \phi$, the total utility changes for both groups become positive.

We analyze the impact of admitting more immigrants on the wages and utility of immigrants under the defined pension replacement rate of the PAYG pension system (the DR pension system). This involves using Eq. (12-c) as the budget constraint of

Table 6-b The effects of admitting immigrants on the wages and utility of immigrants under the DC pension system

Immigrants								
	(A) $\phi =$ 1.00		(B) $\phi =$ 0.82		(C) $\phi =$ 0.52		(D) $\phi =$ – 0.05	
Total utility change		– 0.469%		– 13.641%		0.928%		10.82%
	Wage (%)	Utility (%)	Wage (%)	Utility (%)	Wage (%)	Utility (%)	Wage (%)	Utility (%)
1	0.00	0.00	0.00	0.00	0.00	0.00	0.00	0.00
2	0.00	– 0.06	0.00	0.10	0.00	0.61	0.00	5.69
3	**– 0.99**	**– 0.26**	**– 25.98**	**– 13.62**	**– 53.89**	**0.00**	**– 77.10**	**0.00**
4	– 0.50	– 0.15	– 0.30	– 0.12	0.54	0.32	4.42	5.13
5	0.00	0.00	0.00	0.00	0.00	0.00	0.00	0.00
6	0.00	0.00	0.00	0.00	0.00	0.00	0.00	0.00
7	0.00	0.00	0.00	0.00	0.00	0.00	0.00	0.00
8	0.00	0.00	0.00	0.00	0.00	0.00	0.00	0.00
9	0.00	0.00	0.00	0.00	0.00	0.00	0.00	0.00
10	0.00	0.00	0.00	0.00	0.00	0.00	0.00	0.00

Notes The note in Table 6-a provides instructions on how to interpret the table

the pension system. The outcomes of this analysis are presented in Tables 8-a and 8-b.

Under the DR pension system, the fundamental findings align with those observed under the DC pension system. If the parameters meet the condition $(1 - \delta) < \phi$, the total utility changes for both natives and immigrants become negative. Conversely, when $(1 - \delta) > \phi$, the total utility changes for both groups turn positive.

Tables 6-a, 6-b, 7-a, 7-b, 8-a, 8-b demonstrate that the impact on wages remains consistent across all pension schemes. Nonetheless, the variation in results across different pension schemes indicates that the impacts are scheme-dependent. Generally, the total change in utility for both natives and immigrants is positive. However, it is noteworthy that the utility level of the third generation remains unaffected, whereas other generations experience positive effects upon admitting immigrants. This observation is intriguing, as the third generation, being directly impacted by immigration, does not exhibit any positive or negative changes, in contrast to the other generations.

In the subsequent analysis, we compare which pension scheme is more advantageous for each value of ϕ. Generally, the DR (DB) pension system is more favorable when the wages of natives decrease (increase) due to immigration. Based on this

Table 7-a The effects of admitting immigrants on the wages and utility of natives under the DB pension system

Natives								
	(A) $\phi =$ 1.00		(B) $\phi =$ 0.82		(C) $\phi =$ 0.52		(D) $\phi =$ – 0.05	
Total utility change		– 1.083%		– 0.624%		2.012%		6.772%
	Wage (%)	Utility (%)	Wage (%)	Utility (%)	Wage (%)	Utility (%)	Wage (%)	Utility (%)
1	0.00	0.00	0.00	0.00	0.00	0.00	0.00	0.00
2	0.00	0.14	0.00	0.23	0.00	0.53	0.00	1.80
3	**– 1.02**	**– 1.19**	**– 1.05**	**– 1.15**	**0.27**	**0.53**	**35.71**	**0.00**
4	– 0.50	– 0.03	– 0.28	0.30	0.53	1.49	4.38	4.97
5	0.00	0.00	0.00	0.00	0.00	0.00	0.00	0.00
6	0.00	0.00	0.00	0.00	0.00	0.00	0.00	0.00
7	0.00	0.00	0.00	0.00	0.00	0.00	0.00	0.00
8	0.00	0.00	0.00	0.00	0.00	0.00	0.00	0.00
9	0.00	0.00	0.00	0.00	0.00	0.00	0.00	0.00
10	0.00	0.00	0.00	0.00	0.00	0.00	0.00	0.00

Notes The note to Table 6-a provides instructions on how to interpret this table

analysis, the DR pension system emerges as the most suitable option for both natives and immigrants.[24]

4.2 Discussion

In this section, we examine the mechanism by which the defined replacement rate (DR) pension system becomes preferable when the relationship between natives and immigrants is relatively complementary (substitutable).

Firstly, let's review the characteristics of each pension system. Under the DC pension system, the pension contribution rate is fixed. Generally, an increase in the labor force raises pension benefits but does not affect disposable income, provided the wages of the labor force generation remain unchanged. If the admission of more immigrants leads to higher wages for natives, both disposable income and pension benefits increase. However, since the pension contribution rate is fixed, a portion of the wage increase is transferred from the working generation to the retired generation,

[24] According to Table 4, Case (A) or (B) is identified as the most reasonable scenario for Japan. Consequently, the DR pension system is deemed the most preferable option for natives in Japan.

Table 7-b The effects of admitting immigrants on the wages and utility of immigrants under the DB pension system

Immigrants								
	(A) $\phi =$ 1.00		(B) $\phi =$ 0.82		(C) $\phi =$ 0.52		(D) $\phi =$ – 0.05	
Total utility change		– 0.699%		– 13.976%		2.636%		23.35%
	Wage (%)	Utility (%)	Wage (%)	Utility (%)	Wage (%)	Utility (%)	Wage (%)	Utility (%)
1	0.00	0.00	0.00	0.00	0.00	0.00	0.00	0.00
2	0.00	0.08	0.00	0.17	0.00	0.62	0.00	5.67
3	**– 0.99**	**– 0.76**	**– 25.98**	**– 14.40**	**– 53.89**	**0.00**	**– 77.10**	**0.00**
4	– 0.50	– 0.02	– 0.30	0.25	0.54	2.01	4.42	17.69
5	0.00	0.00	0.00	0.00	0.00	0.00	0.00	0.00
6	0.00	0.00	0.00	0.00	0.00	0.00	0.00	0.00
7	0.00	0.00	0.00	0.00	0.00	0.00	0.00	0.00
8	0.00	0.00	0.00	0.00	0.00	0.00	0.00	0.00
9	0.00	0.00	0.00	0.00	0.00	0.00	0.00	0.00
10	0.00	0.00	0.00	0.00	0.00	0.00	0.00	0.00

Notes The note to Table 6-a provides instructions on how to interpret this table

implying that the disposable income for the working generation doesn't rise as much as the wages do. Therefore, under this system, an increase in the labor force tends to benefit the retired generation more than the working generation.

In the DB and DR pension systems, the pension contribution rate varies with the size of the labor force. Specifically, under the DB system, an increase in the labor force reduces the pension contribution rate but doesn't affect pension benefits. Consequently, this system tends to favor the working generation over the retired generation.

Conversely, in the DR pension system, both pension benefits and contribution rates are affected by the labor force size as they may change proportionally to the wage changes of the working generation, even if the replacement ratio of benefits to wages remains constant. An increase in a relatively complementary labor force could decrease the pension contribution rate, thereby raising the savings rate and wages of the next generation of natives and immigrants. Hence, under the DR system, an increase in a relatively complementary labor force is more beneficial to the working and future generations than to the retired generation.

When the number of relatively more complementary immigrants increases, it raises the wages of natives during the period these immigrants are admitted. Under the DB pension system, a rise in natives' wages lowers the pension contribution rate, increasing disposable income and, consequently, the savings and utility of

Table 8-a The effects of admitting immigrants on the wages and utility of natives under the DR pension system

Natives								
	(A) $\phi = 1.00$		(B) $\phi = 0.82$		(C) $\phi = 0.52$		(D) $\phi = -0.05$	
Total utility change		– 0.373%		– 0.036%		1.944%		6.807%
	Wage (%)	Utility (%)	Wage (%)	Utility (%)	Wage (%)	Utility (%)	Wage (%)	Utility (%)
1	0.00	0.00	0.00	0.00	0.00	0.00	0.00	0.00
2	0.00	0.07	0.00	0.17	0.00	0.50	0.00	1.96
3	**– 1.02**	**– 0.47**	**– 1.05**	**– 0.54**	**0.27**	**0.00**	**35.71**	**0.00**
4	– 0.50	0.02	– 0.28	0.33	0.53	1.44	4.38	4.84
5	0.00	0.00	0.00	0.00	0.00	0.00	0.00	0.00
6	0.00	0.00	0.00	0.00	0.00	0.00	0.00	0.00
7	0.00	0.00	0.00	0.00	0.00	0.00	0.00	0.00
8	0.00	0.00	0.00	0.00	0.00	0.00	0.00	0.00
9	0.00	0.00	0.00	0.00	0.00	0.00	0.00	0.00
10	0.00	0.00	0.00	0.00	0.00	0.00	0.00	0.00

Notes The note to Table 6-a provides instructions on how to interpret this table

future generations. Therefore, the DB pension system is preferred when the admitted immigrants are relatively complementary.

As Collado and Valera (2004) observed, admitting a greater number of immigrants can significantly ease the fiscal burden on future generations in countries with aging populations. This chapter further demonstrates that the productivity relationship between natives and immigrants, along with the chosen pension system, plays a vital role when countries with aging populations admit immigrants.

Table 8-b The effects of admitting immigrants on the wages and utility of immigrants under the DR pension system

Immigrants								
	(A) $\phi =$ 1.00		(B) $\phi =$ – 0.82		(C) $\phi =$ 0.52		(D) $\phi =$ – 0.05	
Total utility change		– 0.360%		– 13.328%		2.563%		22.93%
	Wage (%)	Utility (%)	Wage (%)	Utility (%)	Wage (%)	Utility (%)	Wage (%)	Utility (%)
1	0.00	0.00	0.00	0.00	0.00	0.00	0.00	0.00
2	0.00	– 0.06	0.00	0.10	0.00	0.61	0.00	5.69
3	**– 0.99**	**– 0.31**	**– 25.98**	**– 13.71**	**– 53.89**	**0.00**	**– 77.10**	**0.00**
4	– 0.50	0.01	– 0.30	0.28	0.54	1.95	4.42	17.24
5	0.00	0.00	0.00	0.00	0.00	0.00	0.00	0.00
6	0.00	0.00	0.00	0.00	0.00	0.00	0.00	0.00
7	0.00	0.00	0.00	0.00	0.00	0.00	0.00	0.00
8	0.00	0.00	0.00	0.00	0.00	0.00	0.00	0.00
9	0.00	0.00	0.00	0.00	0.00	0.00	0.00	0.00
10	0.00	0.00	0.00	0.00	0.00	0.00	0.00	0.00

Notes The note to Table 6-a provides instructions on how to interpret this table

5 Conclusion

This study delves into the impact of admitting immigrants on the welfare of native residents, particularly in an economy where native and immigrant labor are imperfect substitutes. This setting includes a PAYG pension system and an education system burdened by the additional requirements of supporting immigrant children. The analysis presented in this chapter highlights that admitting immigrants, even those not perfectly complementary, can potentially increase the wages and utility of natives. Moreover, it points out that the suitability of a pension system is contingent on the nature of the relationship between natives and immigrants.

Significantly, the findings of this chapter, especially when considering the educational burden of immigrant children, show a notable divergence from the conclusions of Razin and Sadka (2000). This underscores the importance of acknowledging the imperfect substitutability between native and immigrant labor. Additionally, our analysis indicates that the benefits accrued to different generations can vary based on the pension system implemented. It is critical to note that an improvement in wage rates does not automatically translate to enhanced welfare for the old generation when admitting immigrants.

While this analysis provides valuable insights, it also acknowledges existing gaps and areas for further investigation. These include the impact on unemployment, as explored by Jinno and Yasuoka (2022), and the endogeneity of educational choices, as discussed by Casarico and Devillanova (2003). It would be desirable to further expand the analysis to include differences in preferences for children between immigrants and native citizens, not only in terms of native residents versus foreign workers but also between skilled and unskilled immigrants. Additionally, considerations such as the extent to which a country's economic welfare includes immigrants (whether they provide only short-term labor supply or long-term residence) and differences in preferences for immigration between younger and older generations should be addressed. These aspects represent important dimensions in understanding the full spectrum of consequences stemming from immigration in the context of an aging economy with a PAYG pension system.

References

Auerbach, A. J., and Oreopoulos, P. (2000). The fiscal impact of us immigration: A generational accounting perspective, In J. Poterba (Ed.), *Tax policy and the economy*, Vol. 14, pp. 124–156. MIT Press.

Bansak, C., Simpson, N., and Zavodny, M. (2021). *The economics of immigration* (2nd ed.). Routledge.

Bernhofer, J., and Tonin, M. (2022). The effect of the language of instruction on academic performance. *Labour Economics*, Vol.*78*, 102218.

Borjas, G. J. (2003). The labor demand curve is downward sloping: Reexamining the impact of immigration on the labor market. *Quarterly Journal of Economics*, Vol. 118, pp. 1335–1374.

Borjas, G. J., and Katz, L. F. (2007). The evolution of the Mexican-born workforce in the United States. In G. J. Borjas (Ed.), *Mexican immigration to the United States*, pp. 13–56. University of Chicago Press.

Brunello, G., Lodigiani, E., and Rocco, L. (2020). Does low skilled immigration increase the education of natives? Evidence from Italian provinces. *Labour Economics*, Vol. 63, pp. 43–54.

Card, D. (2009). Immigration and Inequality. *American Economic Review*, Vol. 99(2), pp. 1–21.

Casarico, A., and Devillanova, C. (2003). Social security and migration with endogenous skill upgrading. *Journal of Public Economics*, Vol. 87, pp. 773–97.

Collado, M. D., Iturbe-Ormaetxe, I., and Valera, G. (2004). Quantifying the impact of immigration on the Spanish welfare state. *International Tax and Public Finance*, Vol. 11, pp. 335–353.

Dustmann, C., and Görlach, J.-S. (2016). The economics of temporary migrations. *Journal of Economic Literature*, Vol. 54(1), pp. 98–136.

Dustmann, C., Schönberg, U., and Stuhler, J. (2016) The impact of immigration: Why do studies reach such different results? *Journal of Economic Perspectives*, Vol. 30(4), pp. 31–56.

Dustmann, C., Frattini, T., and Preston, I. P. (2013) The effect of immigration along the distribution of wages. *Review of Economic Studies*, Vol. 80, pp. 145–173.

Guerreiro, J., Rebelo, S., and Teles, P. (2020). What is the optimal immigration policy? Migration, jobs, and welfare. *Journal of Monetary Economics*, Vol. 113, pp. 61–87.

Immigration Services Agency of Japan. (2024). *Statistics on foreign nationals residing in Japan (as of 31 December 2023)* [in Japanese]. Ministry of Justice. Retrieved June 30, 2025, from https://www.e-stat.go.jp/en/statistics/00250012.

Imrohoroğlu, S., Kitao, S., and Yamada, T. (2017). Can guest workers solve Japan's fiscal problems? *Economic Inquiry*, *55*(3), 1287-1307.

Japan Institute for Labour Policy and Training. (2023). *Databook of international labour statistics.* (No. 35). JILPT.

Japanese Law Transformation. (n.d.). *Immigration control and refugee recognition act.* (Act No. 319 of 1951, as amended). Retrieved June 30, 2025, from https://www.japaneselawtranslation.go.jp/en/laws/view/3624

Jinno, M. (2011). Assimilation, immigration, and the welfare state. *FinanzArchiv*, Vol. 67(1), pp. 46–63.

Jinno, M. (2013). The impact of immigration under the defined-benefit pension system: An analysis incorporating assimilation costs. *Demographic Research*, Vol. 28, pp. 613–36.

Jinno, M., and Yasuoka, M. (2022). Economic benefits of immigration for natives: The effects of immigrants through the school system. *International Review of Economics*, Vol. 69, pp. 125–143.

Jinno, M., and Yasuoka, M. (2024). Effects of relaxing residence status for foreign workers on native residents. *MPRA paper*, 120568, pp. 1–30.

Kato, R. R. (2022). Population aging and labor mobility in Japan. *Japan and The World Economy*, Vol. 62, 101130.

Kemnitz, A. (2003). Immigration, unemployment and pensions. *Scandinavian Journal of Economics*, Vol. 105(1), pp. 31–47.

Korekawa, Y. (2023). Fertility of immigrant women in Japan analysis using the own-children method based on micro-data from the population census of Japan *IPSS Working Paper Series*, Vol. 65, pp. 1–24.

Kosaki, T. (2018). *Rōdōryoku busoku no keizaigaku: Nihon keizai wa dō kawaru ka* [The economics of labor shortage: How will Japan's economy change?] (in Japanese). Tokyo: Nippon Hyōron Sha.

Lee, R., and Miller, T. (2000). Immigration, social security, and broader fiscal impacts. *American Economic Review*, Vol. 90(2), pp. 350–54.

Llull, J. (2020). The impact of immigration on productivity,. In E. Vella, J. Caballé, and J. Llull (Eds.), *Understanding migration with macroeconomics* (pp. 27–58). Palgrave Macmillan.

Mavisakalyan, A. (2011). Immigration, public education spending, and private schooling. *Southern Economic Journal*, Vol. 78(2), pp. 397–423.

Ministry of Education, Culture, Sports, Science and Technology. (2022). *Statistical Abstract 2022* [in Japanese & English]. Retrieved June 30, 2025, from https://www.mext.go.jp/en/publication/statistics/index.htm

Ministry of Education, Culture, Sports, Science & Technology. (2023). NihongoShido ga Hitsuyon-ajidoseito no Ukeirejokyoto ni kansuru Chosa (Reiwa 5-nendo) [Results of the FY2023 survey on the enrollment status of students requiring Japanese language instruction, in Japanese]. Retrieved June 30, 2025, from https://www.mext.go.jp/b_menu/houdou/31/09/1421569_00004.htm

Ministry of Health, Labour and Welfare. (2020). *2019 Basic Survey on Wage Structure: Summary of results* [in Japanese, Data set]. Retrieved June 30, 2025 from https://www.e-stat.go.jp/stat-search/files?page=1&toukei=00450091&tstat=000001011429.

Ministry of Health, Labour and Welfare. (2021). "Gaikokujin koyō jōkyō" no todoke-de jōkyō matome [Status of foreign workers' employment: Summary report, in Japanese] (as of 31 Oct 2020). Retrieved June 30, 2025, from https://www.mhlw.go.jp/content/11655000/000729116.pdf

Nakamura, J., Naito, H., Kambayashi, R., Kawaguchi, D., and Machikita, T. (2009). Nippon no gaikokujin roudou [*Foreign workforce in Japan,* in Japanese]. Nippon Hyoron Sha.

OECD. (2013). *PISA 2012 results: What makes schools successful? Resources, policies and practices (Volume IV).* OECD Publishing.

OECD. (2016). *Low-performing students: Why they fall behind and how to help them succeed.* OECD Publishing.

OECD. (2019). *PISA 2018 results (Volume II): Where all students can succeed.* OECD Publishing.

OECD. (2020). *PISA 2018 results (Volume V): Effective policies, successful schools.* OECD Publishing.

Oh, Y. (2019). Ōrudokamā: Sono rekishi ga toi kakeru mono [Oldcomers: Questions raised by their history]. In Nukaga, M., Shibano, J., & Miura, A. (Eds.), *Imin kara kyōiku o kangaeru:*

Kodomo-tachi o torimaku gurōbaru jidai no kadai [Rethinking education from immigration: Challenges facing children in a global era, in Japanese], pp. 17–28. Nakanishiya Shuppan.
Okamoto, A. (2021). Immigration policy and demographic dynamics: Welfare Analysis of an aging Japan. *Journal of The Japanese and International Economics*, Vol. 62, 101168.
Ottaviano, G. I. P., and Peri, G. (2008). Immigration and national wages: Clarifying the theory and the empirics. *NBER Working Paper*, 14188.
Ottaviano, G. I. P., and Peri, G. (2012). Rethinking the effect of immigration on wages. *Journal of the European Economic Association*, Vol. 10, pp. 152–97.
Powell, B. (2015). *The economics of immigration-market-based approaches, social science, and public policy*. Oxford University Press.
Razin, A., and Sadka, E. (1999). Migration and pension with international capital mobility. *Journal of Public Economics*, Vol. 74(1), pp. 141–50.
Razin, A., and Sadka, E. (2000). Unskilled migration: A burden or a boon for the welfare state? *The Scandinavian Journal of Economics*, Vol. 102(3), pp. 463–79.
Shimasawa, M., and Oguro, K. (2010). Impact of immigration on the Japanese economy: A multi-country simulation model. *Journal of The Japanese and International Economics*, Vol. 24, pp. 586–602.
Silas, A. (2020). *The migrant pay gap: Understanding wage differences between migrants and nationals*. International Labour Office.
Speciale, B. (2012). Does immigration affect public education expenditures? Quasi-experimental evidence. *Journal of Public Economics*, Vol. 96, pp. 773–83.
Statistics Bureau, Ministry of Internal Affairs and Communications. (2020, December 1). *Labour Force Survey (Basic Tabulation), October 2020 results* [in Japanese]. e-Stat. Retrieved June 30, 2025, from https://www.stat.go.jp/data/roudou/rireki/tsuki/pdf/202010.pdf
Statistics Bureau, Ministry of Internal Affairs and Communications. (2022). *Labour Force Survey: 2021 annual average results*. e-Stat. Retrieved June 30, 2025, from https://www.e-stat.go.jp/en/stat-search/files?layout=dataset&toukei=00200531&tstat=000001226891&year=20210
Storesletten, K. (2000). Sustaining fiscal policy through immigration. *Journal of Political Economy, 108*(2), 300–23.
The Japan Times. (2022). Japan may allow 10,000 people per day to enter country from April. Retrieved December 7, 2023, from https://www.japantimes.co.jp/news/2022/03/15/national/entry-arrivals-raised/
Valbuena, J., Mediavilla, M., Choi, Á., and Gil, M. (2021). Effects of grade retention policies: A literature review of empirical studies applying causal inference. *Journal of Economic Surveys*, Vol. 35(2), 408–451.
United Nations Department of Economic and Social Affairs, Population Division. (2020). *International migration 2020 highlights.*
Zinovyeva, N., Felgueroso, F., and Vazquez, P. (2014). Immigration and student achievement in Spain: Evidence from PISA. *SERIEs: Journal of the Spanish Economic Association*, Vol. 5, pp. 25–60.

Masaya Yasuoka is a professor at the School of Economics, Kwansei Gakuin University. His main areas of research interest are public finance, social security, and macroeconomics. He has published papers in scholarly journals including *Economics Letters, Economic Modelling, International Review of Economics* and *Journal of the Economics of Ageing*. Professor Yasuoka received a B.A. in economics from Nagoya City University and a Ph.D. in economics from Kobe University.

Masatoshi Jinno is a professor in the Faculty of Economics at Nanzan University. His research centers on immigration economics, public pension and social-security finance, and education economics. He has published articles in journals such as *FinanzArchiv: Public Finance Analysis*, *Demographic Research*, *The Singapore Economic Review*, and *The International Review of Economics*. He earned a Ph.D. in Economics from Nagoya University and holds a B.A. in Foreign Studies from Osaka University of Foreign Studies.

MIX
Papier aus verantwortungsvollen Quellen
Paper from responsible sources
FSC® C105338

If you have any concerns about our products,
you can contact us on
ProductSafety@springernature.com

In case Publisher is established outside the EU,
the EU authorized representative is:
Springer Nature Customer Service Center GmbH
Europaplatz 3, 69115 Heidelberg, Germany

Printed by Libri Plureos GmbH
in Hamburg, Germany